THE Tree Doctor

THE Tree Doctor

A Guide to Tree Care and Maintenance

DANIEL PRENDERGAST   ERIN PRENDERGAST

FIREFLY BOOKS

A FIREFLY BOOK

Published by Firefly Books Ltd. 2017
Copyright © 2017 Firefly Books Ltd.
Text copyright © 2017 Daniel Prendergast and Erin Prendergast

First printing

Publisher Cataloging-in-Publication Data (U.S.)
A CIP record for this title is available from Library of Congress

Library and Archives Canada Cataloguing in Publication
A CIP record for this title is available from Library and Archives Canada

Published in the United States by
Firefly Books (U.S.) Inc.
P.O. Box 1338, Ellicott Station
Buffalo, New York 14205

Published in Canada by
Firefly Books Ltd.
50 Staples Avenue, Unit 1
Richmond Hill, Ontario L4B 0A7

Cover and interior design: LINDdesign

Printed in China

This book has been printed
on FSC® certified paper.

We acknowledge the financial support
of the Government of Canada.

CONTENTS

We dedicate this book to our parents and siblings,

and to all those who love trees.

Time spent under a shade tree on a hot summer day is peaceful, but also cooler. The hot air is cooled as it moves through the tree's canopy.

THE BENEFITS OF TREES

FOR MANY OF US, trees are a constant force in our lives. They flourish in our backyards, city streets and neighborhood parks, lending an air of humble nobility to the frenetic pace of our daily routines. In northern climates, the changing characteristics of deciduous trees signal the arrival of new seasons. The blazing foliage of red, orange and yellow leaves sheds with the approach of winter, and fresh **buds** and green growth appear during spring, a time of renewed life. In the south, the live oak, a popular and characteristic **shade tree**, remains stately and vibrant all year long. Many tree species throughout Canada and the United States, such as the giant Douglas fir of the Pacific Northwest, the flowering magnolia of the Deep South and the syrup-producing sugar maple of the Northeast, are cherished symbols of home, valued for their distinct features, their strength and their beauty.

The International Society of Arboriculture (ISA), the largest and most influential organization of its kind, serves the tree-care industry as a scientific and educational organization. The ISA has published a brochure on the benefits of trees, which are outlined in this chapter.

Tree owners know that the impact that trees have on a landscape transcends their size and stature. Trees make life pleasant for us and also offer social benefits.

Time spent amidst a grove of trees is often relaxing. While painters and writers have been inspired by the aesthetic and spiritual appeal of trees, hospital patients have been known to recover from surgery more quickly when their rooms offer views of trees. We see the strong ties between people and trees when community residents protest the removal of trees to widen city streets and when individuals make valiant efforts to save large or historic trees. Trees benefit our communities by bringing groups together in neighborhood plantings.

+ By planting trees in our cities, we help create a more natural environment that attracts birds and other wildlife to the area. Natural cycles of plant growth, reproduction and decomposition are present, both above- and belowground. Harmony and balance are restored to the urban landscape.

Reversing the Heat Island

Homeowners can reverse the effects of the city as a heat island by planting more trees and increasing the urban forest cover, which can help to make a city more livable and protect the health of its residents. If you're concerned about the environment, you can make a difference by planting a tree.

Many cities throughout North America encourage community commitment to trees. Learn more about tree planting in your area by contacting your local municipal representatives or visiting online resources such as the Arbor Day Foundation/Tree City USA website: www.arborday.org.

Some cities encourage expansion of urban forestry canopies by offering free trees for planting on city-owned land in front of your property. Consider taking advantage of such programs.

The urban forests in ravines, parks and residential neighborhoods help improve the quality of city life for all inhabitants.

We often become personally attached to trees — and why not? Trees are fun! No play equipment will ever replace a good climbing tree. Trees add color, form and dimension to our gardens. They are our steadfast companions, lasting for lifetimes.

Because of their potential for long lives, trees are frequently planted as living memorials, establishing links to our past. Counted among the Earth's longest living and largest organisms, many trees last between 100 and 200 years, or even longer. The eastern hemlock, for example, can live between 600 and 1,000 years. Even smaller trees, which are considered short-lived, typically survive between 60 and 80 years.

In addition to providing social benefits, trees alter the environment in which we live by moderating the climate, improving air quality, conserving water and providing refuge to wildlife.

Trees help make our city streets more aesthetically pleasing and natural looking. Trees help prevent soil erosion in hills and ravines, and along waterways. Trees also support an underground network of life, which helps keep the soil around them healthy.

Radiant energy from the sun is absorbed or deflected by leaves on deciduous trees in the summer and is filtered by their branches during the winter. Trees also combat wind speed — the more compact the **foliage** on the trees or group of trees, the greater the influence of the windbreak — and have an impressive ability to muffle noise. Leaves and small branches act as baffles, absorbing and deflecting sound. Trees divert the downward fall of rain; they also intercept water and store some of it, thereby reducing storm runoff and the possibility of flooding.

Leaves filter the air we breathe by removing dust and other particles. They absorb carbon dioxide from the air to form carbohydrates that are used in the structure and function of woody plants. In this process, leaves also absorb other air pollutants, such as ozone, carbon monoxide and sulfur dioxide. The combined chemistry of the thousands of leaves on each tree eliminates an enormous volume of pollutants from the air. After processing all of the chemicals, trees give off water and oxygen.

The Benefits of Trees

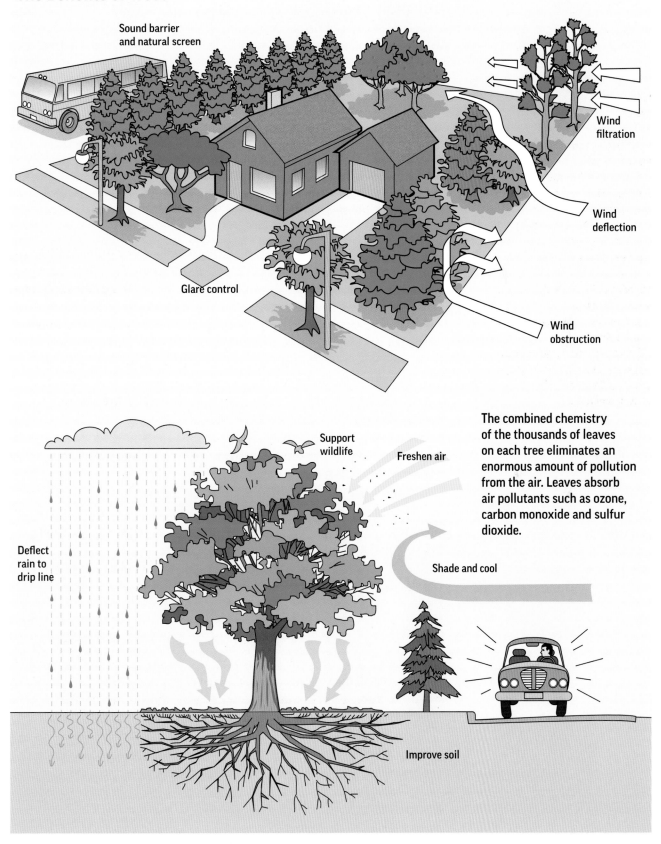

Sound barrier and natural screen

Wind filtration

Wind deflection

Wind obstruction

Glare control

Deflect rain to drip line

Support wildlife

Freshen air

The combined chemistry of the thousands of leaves on each tree eliminates an enormous amount of pollution from the air. Leaves absorb air pollutants such as ozone, carbon monoxide and sulfur dioxide.

Shade and cool

Improve soil

The presence of trees on residential lots brings life and energy to paved streets.

On average, woody plants add between 5 and 7 percent to the value of a residential lot.

Trees benefit all areas of life

The benefits of trees are impressive and far-reaching.
- Social: Trees have the power to quiet our souls and to connect us to one another. They add civility to the harsh environs of urban life.
- Environmental: Trees cool and clean the air, deflect wind, muffle noise and improve soil conditions.
- Economic: Trees help decrease electricity bills and increase the value of real estate.

A mature maple or oak tree transpires 82 gallons of moisture every 24 hours. A great redwood transpires approximately 500 gallons of moisture per day. This moisture eventually takes the form of dew or rain. Trees draw upon the deep groundwater, thereby lifting water tables and maintaining moisture in the surrounding topsoil.

Even belowground, trees are doing beneficial things for the landscape. Tree roots anchor the tree in the ground, soak up water and nutrients from the soil, prevent the soil from eroding and support an underground universe of beneficial insects and organisms, which, in turn, keep the soil around them healthy and teeming with life.

Trees are efficient at cooling the air. The air cools as water vapor evaporates from tree leaves, which explains why it feels fresh and cool under a tree on a hot day.

Shade trees are tremendous assets for urban communities. When the sun beats down on barren concrete, asphalt and glass, cities heat up to 9 degrees Fahrenheit warmer than their rural counterparts, creating a

Trees in urban areas help ensure the continued presence of wildlife, including healthy bird populations.

In addition to offering shade for animals, trees planted in farmers' fields also create windbreaks, which reduce wind and soil erosion.

The Arbor Day Foundation encourages farmers, ranchers and acreage owners to plant trees as an integral component of production agriculture. Conversation trees improve crop yields and preserve topsoil for future abundant harvests. They also prevent erosion and clean the water when planted along streams and wetlands. In marginal areas of agricultural land, trees attract wildlife, sequester carbon and help with flood control.

phenomenon known as the **heat island effect**. These surfaces retain heat and continue to radiate stored heat back into the atmosphere well into the evening, making it feel warmer than it does outside the city limits.

Shade trees can cool individual neighborhoods and entire cities by preventing the heat island effect in two ways: in the heat of summer, temperatures are 10 degrees Fahrenheit cooler under the shade of a mature tree and, as wind moves air through a shade canopy, it is cooled. A stand of trees, therefore, can create a welcoming **oasis effect**.

Trees planted effectively will also help you to save money and conserve energy. One of the best means of conserving energy is by planting windbreaks. Living windbreaks of trees can do much to keep our soil productive and to improve our environment. They also reduce or eliminate the undesirable effects of excessive wind velocities.

The direct economic benefits provided by trees are usually associated with energy costs. By providing good protection from winds, trees can reduce winter heating costs and summer cooling costs by 25 to 30 percent. Trees also provide indirect economic benefits to communities. For example, customers will receive lower electricity bills when power companies use less water in their cooling towers, build fewer new facilities to meet peak demands, use reduced amounts of fossil fuels in their furnaces and need to take fewer measures to control air pollution. Communities also save money when fewer facilities are built to control storm water in the region.

Trees have a considerable impact on real estate values. Healthy, mature trees can add 20 percent or more to the value of a residential property. Studies show that people are willing to pay 3 to 7 percent more for a house in a well-treed neighborhood. According to the International Society of Arboriculture, property values of landscaped properties are 5 to 20 percent higher than those of non-landscaped properties.

Municipal trees often serve both architectural and engineering functions. They provide privacy, emphasize views or screen out unsightly ones, reduce glare and reflection, and direct pedestrian traffic. Their

Trees Help Combat the Climate Crisis

TREES ARE THE MOST prominent organisms on our planet, helping our local ecosystems and Earth as a whole by capturing and storing heat-trapping carbon dioxide and combating human-made climate change. Trees (and shrubs) have woody stems that are long-lasting and grow bigger every year, which makes them good for storing carbon.

Our planet has become greener in the past decade. According to a study led by a group of scholars at Australian, Chinese, Dutch and Saudi Arabian universities and published in the journal *Nature Climate Change*, there has been a gain in the world's carbon-absorbing green matter. Following a decline between 1998 and 2002 — due largely to deforestation in the tropical rain forests of Brazil and Indonesia — the Earth's green matter increased between 2003 and 2012. Deforestation in Brazil and Indonesia slowed sharply, conditions improved in northern Australia and southern Africa and, most dramatically, the vast forests of China and Russia grew back. This is significant because the boreal forest, which stretches across Northern Canada and Russia, stores almost 60 percent of the world's carbon (tropical forests store about half that much).

This study, like others, shows that the share of carbon emissions caused by deforestation has declined in the past decade. Countries have initiated policies to create conditions for more carbon-friendly ecology. In the 1990s, the European Union introduced programs to return former croplands to forest. China's reforestation program, known as the Great Green Wall, intends to replant almost 400 million hectares of forest in a vast strip across northern China by 2050, making it the world's largest reforestation program. In 2004, Brazil launched an action plan for the prevention and control of deforestation in the Amazon, which has helped the deforestation rate fall by almost 80 percent. At the United Nations Climate Change Conference in Paris in 2015, broad efforts were agreed upon to ensure the continuing role of forests in preserving a livable planet. This commitment reflects the growing recognition that ending forest loss and allowing forests to regrow are essential to limiting the risks of global warming.

Studies also conclude that, despite these efforts, there are trillions fewer trees than there used to be. An estimated 15 billion trees are cut down each year and only 5 billion are replanted, resulting in a net annual loss of 10 billion trees. Computer models demonstrate that, before humans, the world had about 5.6 trillion trees. There are currently only approximately 3 trillion trees in existence.

Trees play a significant role in helping to reduce greenhouse gas emissions. However, they are not enough on their own to absorb all of the carbon dioxide emitted through fossil fuel industries. Individuals can affect climate change by reducing their use of fossil fuels (including coal, oil and gas), and trees can play an important role in achieving this goal.

During the hottest summer months, about half of the electricity used in the United States powers air conditioners. Planting trees around buildings provides shade and cools the air through transpiration, offsetting air-conditioning emissions by up to 70 percent. Greener communities are cooler communities. Just three trees, placed effectively around a house, can save up to 30 percent of energy use. Shaded parking lots keep cars cooler, reducing emissions from fuel tanks and engines. Similarly, in the winter months, well-placed trees that slow wind can reduce the energy used for heating by 30 percent, while trees used as snow fences reduce the energy required to plow roads and parking lots.

Oxford University researchers suggest that planting trees where there were none before — known as afforestation — is another promising way to offset climate change. Planting trees benefits the atmosphere and is a comparatively low-cost and low-risk process. In Canada, scientists are experimenting with assisted migration, an effort to plant trees farther north than their seeds would naturally fall in order to extend their range, which helps them, in effect, to flee climate change. This is a controversial practice, given that the ecological effects are unpredictable.

Aerial view of tropical deforestation, Mato Grosso do Sul, Pantanal, Brazil

Volunteers join together and plant young trees in deep mud in a mangrove reforestation project on September 16, 2014, in Samutsakorn, Thailand.

Aerial view of Chicago, Illinois: Maintaining a resilient and diverse urban forest is a key element in being able to adapt to climate change.

Cities and communities are preparing for the impacts of climate change in the coming decades. Some of the following impacts are predicted by Natural Resources Canada:

- warmer winter temperatures;
- changes in precipitation patterns;
- increased storm activity and wind velocity; and
- more extreme events, such as drought and heavy rainfall.

Although the exact nature of these changes is unknown, certain implications can be anticipated:

- increased resources to deal with extreme weather and response;
- expanded care in response to more persistent pests;
- an increased need for watering of drought- and heat-stressed trees; and
- expanded education and emergency planning.

Maintaining a resilient and diverse urban forest is a key element in being able to adapt to climate change, as are preparedness and the ability to respond quickly to change.

Whether you plant trees in your community, on your property or in national forests, doing so will help fight climate change. Trees absorb carbon dioxide and other pollutants through the natural process of photosynthesis, then store the carbon and emit pure oxygen.

presence also complements and enhances buildings and architectural features, much to the delight of city dwellers.

In addition to the material benefits that trees bestow upon urban centers and city inhabitants, they also enhance the appearance of residential homes. Using trees in gardens and landscaped settings provides the opportunity to create, sustain and enjoy an earthly paradise in your own backyard.

The Urban Forest

The urban forest is made up of trees along city streets, trees in parks, ravines and natural areas, trees in front and backyards, and trees in landscaped open spaces such as golf courses, cemeteries and local businesses. The urban forest is a shared resource that benefits the entire community. In addition to its environmental and health benefits, the urban forest also increases property values. Ravines and other treed green spaces are often associated with the highest property values in a city.

Enlightened civic governments in North America recognize the importance and value of a vigorous urban tree canopy. Not only do trees improve the quality of life for city dwellers by offering shade and improved air quality, they are aesthetically pleasing and enhance city streetscapes. Green spaces enhance a city livability rankings and attract the attention worldwide.

Trees, forests and natural areas are essential elements of a healthy city that supports and promotes the well-being of its citizens. The presence of trees and green spaces in a community has been linked to reduced crime rates. It has also been linked to better health in city dwellers. Studies

Trees planted by municipal authorities on busy streets improve a city's world standing; they attract residents, tourists and new businesses. They are a worthy economic investment.

Tree plantings in public spaces like New York City's High Line deeply enrich city life and attract urban dwellers and tourists alike. (Approximately 4.8 million people visited the High Line in 2013.)

Planting Trees in the City

It's important to understand soil conditions, tree biology and landscape design when you're planting trees in the city. As outlined in in the International Society of Arboriculture's publication *Up by Roots: Healthy Soils and Trees in the Built Environment* by James Urban, the following principles may be applied:

1. Plant in the easy places first. Assign large trees to areas where you have the largest or best soil resources.

2. Make larger planting spaces. Reduce paved areas and increase areas open for soil.

3. Preserve and reuse existing soil resources. Removing and replacing soil is destructive to the environment. There are often usable soils at urban sites and, if reasonable soil exists, reusing it is the best option.

4. Improve soil and drainage. Consider deep-tilling any compacted soil and using a **soil amendment**. In the urban landscape, too much water is more problematic than too little.

5. Respect the base of the tree. Do not pave the area around a tree's future trunk flare.

6. Make space for roots. Ensure there is enough space for roots under any pavement.

7. Select the right tree. In addition to aesthetic qualities, you should consider the local climate, maintenance requirements, availability and soil preference.

conducted in various locations in the United Kingdom and the United States concluded that children living in "green neighborhoods" had lower asthma rates and were less likely to be obese than those in less green areas. In the U.K., there were fewer health disparities between high- and low-income populations among families who lived in communities with green surroundings.

Streets lined with trees are desirable places to live and work, and therefore attract residents, businesses and visitors. The presence of trees on city streets is a key aspect of sustainable communities.

Almost all of the benefits of living among trees come from the tree canopy. As trees mature and their canopy opens, they cast a pleasing dappled shade that allows a greater variety of plant life to develop. Larger trees develop tall trunks, enabling vista lines at eye level (as opposed to smaller trees that are thickly branched at lower levels and obscure sight lines). Small trees need to be planted closer together to form a continuous canopy, which takes up valuable ground space and creates more trunk obstructions. Trees that mature to large sizes should be spaced widely wherever possible, as opposed to small varieties that can be planted closer together. An urban scale is evident in larger trees, not smaller ones.

Treed streets and spaces bind communities together. Trees located closer to human activity provide more environmental and cultural benefits than those planted in remote locations. Their canopies absorb dust and reduce energy use, and their roots absorb rainwater. Thus, a tree that shades a building or parking lot does more to mitigate human impact than one that shades only soil.

Ancient Trees and Old-Growth Forests

Few trees in urban and suburban areas live long enough to experience what biologists call the "ancient state" of tree life. During this stage, trees experience retrenchment: their canopy becomes more compact as the **crown** dies back and the tree begins to shed large branches; they are less able to form woundwood when they have been injured; and they put on less new growth after insect attacks or pruning.

Yet, despite extensive decay, ancient trees can still be healthy and vigorous. Trees in this stage of life save a lot of energy because their growth rate is significantly reduced. This may be why some trees live a long time in this phase. Continuous "downsizing" allows them to live for thousands of years. The oldest living organisms in the world — bristlecone pines more than 4,000 years old — grow in the hard mountain environment of California's White Mountains at altitudes higher than 11,000 feet. Other long-living ancient trees include the old-growth redwoods of California, the 2,000-year-old Sitka spruces of the Pacific Northwest, the 1,000-year-old yews and 300- to 400-year-old oaks of the United Kingdom and the centuries-old ginkgoes of Japan.

Life of a Tree

1942 Second World War
1917 First World War
1885 The Canadian Pacific Railway is completed
1778 James Cook lands on Vancouver Island
1608 Quebec City is founded by Samuel de Champlain
1534 Jacques Cartier arrives on the Gaspé Peninsula
1497 John Cabot explores the east coast of Canada
1408 Last record of Viking population
1215 King John signs the Magna Carta
1206 Temujin is proclaimed "Genghis Khan"
1202 Constantinople is captured

Ravines, trails and parks filled with trees provide respite and reprieve from the stresses of the city's fast-paced daily life.

Even if their gnarled appearances mean that they are not conventionally beautiful or that they're no longer valuable sources of timber, ancient trees play an important role as a habitat for wildlife and other living organisms.

Canada's old-growth forests are an environmental treasure and play a significant role in sequestering carbon. Old-growth forests are those that have been undisturbed by natural occurrences or human activity for a long time. They are structurally and ecologically diverse and feature multilayered canopies with various tree species at different stages in their life cycles. Old trees support species that do not occur in younger forests and offer precious habitats for animals and plants. Even after big old trees fall as deadwood, they act as giant reservoirs of carbon, water and nutrient cycling.

People are passionate about trees. In the district of Tofino on Vancouver Island — located on the southern edge of Clayoquot Sound, a UNESCO Biosphere Reserve in the middle of a temperate rainforest — trees are considered treasures. In 2002, residents rallied around an 800-year-old red cedar that was declared hazardous due to inner rot, likening the old, stately tree to a cathedral in Europe. The citizens mobilized, two men lived in the tree's canopy for 37 days and funds were raised to fortify the tree with a steel girdle. For this reason and others — including protesting logging in an old-growth forest in Clayoquot Sound — Tofino is known as the tree-hugging capital of the world.

Having an abundance of trees in urban centers improves the quality of life for all inhabitants, both people and wildlife alike.

Balled-and-burlapped trees are sold with their roots surrounded with a ball of soil wrapped in burlap. They are generally heavy to lift, so you might consider an additional expense of delivery and planting assistance.

TREE
SELECTION
AND PLACEMENT

2

TREES ESTABLISH A LANDSCAPE'S general character more than any other plant. They are the most dominant and permanent elements in our yards and they can determine the framework of our gardens by dictating the amount of sun or shade that enters the space. Trees are awesome landmarks. They can direct sight lines and create perspective. Trees can soften hard architectural lines and link structures to the landscape. They can be used to frame special vistas and black out unattractive ones. Trees can also offer seasonal features, such as bright spring blossoms, showy flowers or fruits, and blazing autumn foliage. A balance of evergreen and deciduous trees provides a variety of color and texture throughout the seasons. When carefully placed, trees can block or divert prevailing winds and absorb or moderate noises outside.

Fortunately, the range of trees available to gardeners is impressive — there are scores of striking tree types from which to choose.

+ What is the difference between a tree and a shrub? Both are woody plants, but shrubs are usually smaller, have branches at ground level and are multi-stemmed. Trees live longer than shrubs.

What Is a Tree?

Simply defined, a tree is a tall woody plant, usually with a single trunk supporting a distinct crown of foliage. (A shrub is also a woody plant, but it is usually smaller and has branches at ground level. Trees live longer than most shrubs.) Trees fall into two basic categories: evergreen (those that have green foliage throughout the year) and deciduous (those that lose their leaves in fall).

Most trees reach between 50 and 80 feet in height, but some grow taller. For example, the eastern white pine can reach up to 100 feet, while the American sycamore, tulip tree and white oak can reach up to 115 feet.

Trees of various sizes, shapes and colors add form, dimension and interest to your landscape.

Evergreens

Evergreen trees and shrubs keep their foliage year-round. Most evergreens – such as pine, spruce and fir trees – have needles. However, there are also evergreens with broad leaves and evergreens with scale-like leaves, such as cedars and junipers. Trees such as pines, spruces and cedars, which produce their seeds within cones, are called **conifers**. Male cones produce pollen, which blows on the wind to reach female cones. Once their pollen is shed, the male cones fall. Seeds then develop within the female cones, which can remain on trees for more than three years. Most conifers are evergreens, although there are some exceptions.

Deciduous

Trees and shrubs that shed all of their foliage during autumn to prepare for dormancy during winter are known as deciduous. (There are some exceptions, like the larch, which is a deciduous conifer, a cone-bearing tree that sheds its soft needles in fall after a display of brilliant yellow foliage.) Large deciduous trees are commonly referred to as **shade trees**.

Small trees such as the pussy willow, mountain maple and poison sumac rarely exceed 16 feet. To support a large trunk and branches, many of a tree's cells are gradually transformed into non-living tissues, such as wood and cork. These dead cells account for approximately 80 percent of a mature tree. The remaining 20 percent comprises live cells that maintain the tree's vital functions.

A **dwarf tree** is a tree that is smaller than the usual size for a particular species. A tree that grows to be 10 feet tall may be considered a dwarf if the usual height of that species is much larger. Dwarf trees grow slowly, only a few inches each year.

What Parts Make Up a Tree?

- The sturdy, woody trunk of a tree supports the weight of the mass aboveground. The trunk also supplies the tree's living tissues with water and nutrients from the ground and with food from the leaves.
- A trunk is made up of several distinct layers, each with a different function.
- The outermost layer is the bark, which forms a protective waterproof layer that can shield the tree from fire damage, insect or fungal attack, and stress from sudden temperature changes.
- All bark has small, round or elongated pores called **lenticels**, which allow the trunk to breathe.
- Bark cells grow from a special thin layer of living cells on the inner side of the bark, called **cork or bark cambium**.
- Each year, the cork cambium lays down a successive layer of bark. As growth continues, the outermost layers of bark are forced to split into ridges or scales, or to peel away (like birch bark).
- On the inner side of the cork cambium lies the **phloem**. This thin layer of cells is very important because it carries food produced by the tree's leaves (in the form of carbohydrates) to all its other living tissues.
- On the inner side of the phloem lies an even narrower ring of cells called the cambium. These cells are responsible for increasing the diameters of the tree's trunk or branches.
- Cambium cells produce phloem cells along the outer surface of the ring and xylem cells along the inner surface. The **xylem cells** transport water, nutrients and oxygen up from the roots to the branches and leaves, where the tree produces food for energy. The cells join and form thousands of elongated capillary tubes that extend up the trunk.
- Most of the rest of the trunk, referred to as **wood**, is made up of dead xylem cells. As long as xylem cells continue to transport fluids, they are part of the tree's **sapwood**. Once they clog and cease to function, they become part of the **heartwood**.

TREE SELECTION AND PLACEMENT

The uniformity of shape and planting distance creates a classical focal point and sight line.

A glossary of terms is provided at the back of this book. Various terms in bold, such as **V-shaped crotch** and **central leader**, are defined in more detail. Please refer to the glossary when you come across a term that requires clarification.

- Heartwood helps support the trunk, but a tree's heartwood can rot away, leaving a hollow trunk, while the branches and leaves of the tree continue to flourish.
- Trees growing in temperate regions, where there are definite seasonal changes in growth, develop patterns in their wood called **annual rings**. These are the rings of wood laid down each year after the burst of spring growth.
- Annual rings may be observed as concentric circles across a log or stump when a tree is cut down or as a series of light and dark bands. Counting these rings reveals the age of the tree.
- We can learn about a tree's history and growth rate through its annual rings because health and environmental factors affect the rings' widths. For example, drought, cold years, insect infestations and pollution can all make a tree produce narrow annual rings. Increased light and warm years can result in wider rings.
- Branches develop the same woody structure as trunks. Young shoots and branches are called twigs.
- In twigs, the soft central cone of early growth, called the **pith**, is more obvious.

The Parts of a Tree

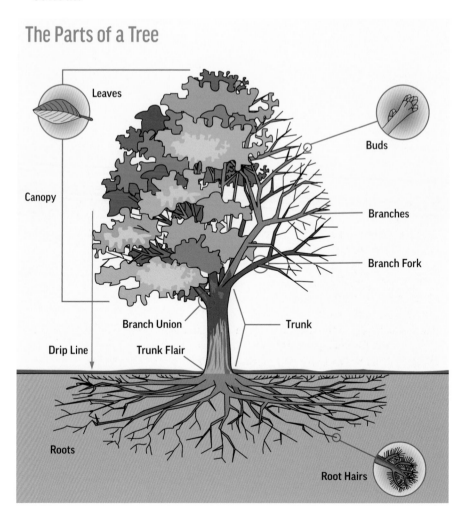

Leaves

Buds

Canopy

Branches

Branch Fork

Branch Union

Trunk

Drip Line

Trunk Flair

Roots

Root Hairs

Trees receive nourishment through their leaves and roots.

Roots

A tree's roots serve four primary functions: anchorage, storage, absorption and conduction. Roots grow near the ground's surface where moisture and oxygen are available, usually in the top 8 to 12 inches of soil. Roots extend outward horizontally from the tree at great distances, often one to two times the height of the tree itself.

Absorbing roots are smaller roots that have fine root hairs, which help in the uptake of water and minerals. The downward-growing taproot of young trees is usually choked out by the expansion of roots around it or is diverted by unfavorable growing conditions. Feeder roots compete directly with the roots of grass and other groundcovers, and provide the major portion of the absorption surface of a tree's root system.

Many trees have fungi called **mycorrhizae** on their roots. These fungi cover the root hairs and help with the absorption process. In turn, the mycorrhizae are fed by the tree roots, forming a symbiotic relationship.

Look for healthy green leaves and bud development.

- Branch tips and twigs grow lengthwise as well as widthwise (although a branch at 3 feet in height will always be 3 feet in height). Recent growth is often shown in leaf or bud scars on young branches. Each summer, small branches produce buds along their lengths and tips. By autumn, each bud contains the rudimentary cells necessary to produce a new structure.
- The tip bud is often much larger than lower side buds or lateral buds. It produces a new extension of the shoot the following year.
- Leaves house the tree's food factories and respiration devices.
- A tree produces food by first capturing the sun's energy with the green pigment **chlorophyll**, concentrated in outer leaf tissues.
- A leaf then uses the trapped energy in a process called **photosynthesis**, which is the combining of carbon dioxide and water to produce sugars and oxygen.
- Leaves take in carbon dioxide and give off moisture and oxygen through their **stomata**, tiny pores in the leaves.

How to Choose a Healthy Tree from a Nursery

To ensure that the tree you buy will be successful on your property when planted, select a vigorous tree. A tree purchased in poor health will likely have more problems, attract insects and require more maintenance. Here are some important signs to look for when choosing a tree, as suggested by the International Society of Arboriculture:

1. Avoid trees with damage to the trunk or with broken branches that have been injured in transport or from equipment.
2. Look for good twig extension growth, which indicates the plant is healthy.
3. Avoid trees with V-shaped crotches, poor branch spacing and upright branches (see page 29, circled).
4. Look for an abundance of healthy green leaves.
5. The tree should have one central leader with spreading branches. Do not purchase a tree that has two **competing leaders**.
6. Look for insects and disease problems on the leaves, branches and trunk.
7. The **root ball** should be solid and well supported within twine or a wire basket. The ball should be moist and protected from drying out.
8. The roots should be white. Roots that are brown or black indicate poor health. Avoid trees with roots that are circling, kinked or **girdling** other roots.

Clockwise from top left:

Balled-and-burlapped trees are sold with their roots surrounded by a ball of soil wrapped in burlap. They are generally heavy to lift, so you might consider paying for delivery and planting assistance.

Container-grown plants like these evergreens are sold in pots filled with soil and already have an established root system.

The root ball should be solid and well-supported with wire or twine. (The circle indicates a V-shaped crotch, something to avoid.)

Make sure the trunk or main stem of the tree appears healthy and has not suffered any damage from transport.

How Trees Are Sold

Container-grown trees are sold in pots filled with soil and have established root systems, which makes them easy to transplant. They are usually more expensive because the plants have been nurtured.

Balled and burlapped young trees are sold with their roots surrounded in balls of soil wrapped in burlap. Even large evergreens, such as spruce and pine trees, are often sold in this manner. It is essential that the root ball be consistently moist. Balled and burlapped trees are sometimes displayed at garden centers in large wooden boxes filled with wood chips. These trees are often too heavy to lift and may require the additional expenses of delivery and mechanical planting.

Bare-root trees are sold with their roots not covered by soil or container. It is important that the roots be kept consistently moist and cool prior to planting. Bare-root trees must not be subjected to freezing temperatures during shipping. These trees are less expensive than container-grown plants and those that are balled and burlapped.

Other Tips to Consider When Purchasing a Tree

Look for your specimen early in the season, before the tree's roots suffer from becoming root-bound, which occurs when trees have been growing in pots all season long.

Signs of root damage include drooping and/or browned **candles** (lighter-colored and softer new growth at the ends of branches) and dry needles with pines and spruces that fall off. If your new tree turns brown shortly after planting, its roots may have been injured before you purchased it. Check with your nursery about its guarantee policy before purchasing a tree.

Trained evergreens, such as junipers or weeping Norway spruces, and **grafted** trees are sold staked; otherwise, these trees would grow flat along the ground. Some young trees are also sold staked so that their trunks stay straight. Don't buy larger trees with scrawny trunks that are staked.

1. The term "field-grown" indicates the tree was raised on a tree farm in a field where it was well-watered with adequate room to grow. If possible, choose field-grown trees when buying a balled and burlapped tree.
2. Nursery-grown trees tend to be thicker and more compact, and have stronger, more vigorous root systems than trees dug out of the wild.

A tree's bark offers a variety of appearances and can be a point of interest in your yard.

Hardiness Rating

The accepted standard of determining the hardiness of a particular plant is called a zone rating. Zone maps are based chiefly on the minimum winter temperatures, but also take other issues into account, such as the length of the growing season, soil conditions and fluctuating temperatures. Canadian plant hardiness zones run from the coldest zone of 0 to the warmest zone of 9. The higher the zone, the greater number of plant species can be grown there. By and large, the Canadian and U.S. zone systems are interchangeable.

Because zone ratings may not accurately reflect the precise conditions in your garden, they should be used as a general guide rather than a hard-and-fast rule. To help determine the zone in your area, call a local garden center or talk to experienced gardeners. Remember that an out-of-zone tree will likely grow slowly and may never attain its potential size.

A native tree naturally suited to the conditions of your site will grow easily, but it will face enormous stress if it is introduced to an environment where the conditions are very different from its native habitat. Some trees

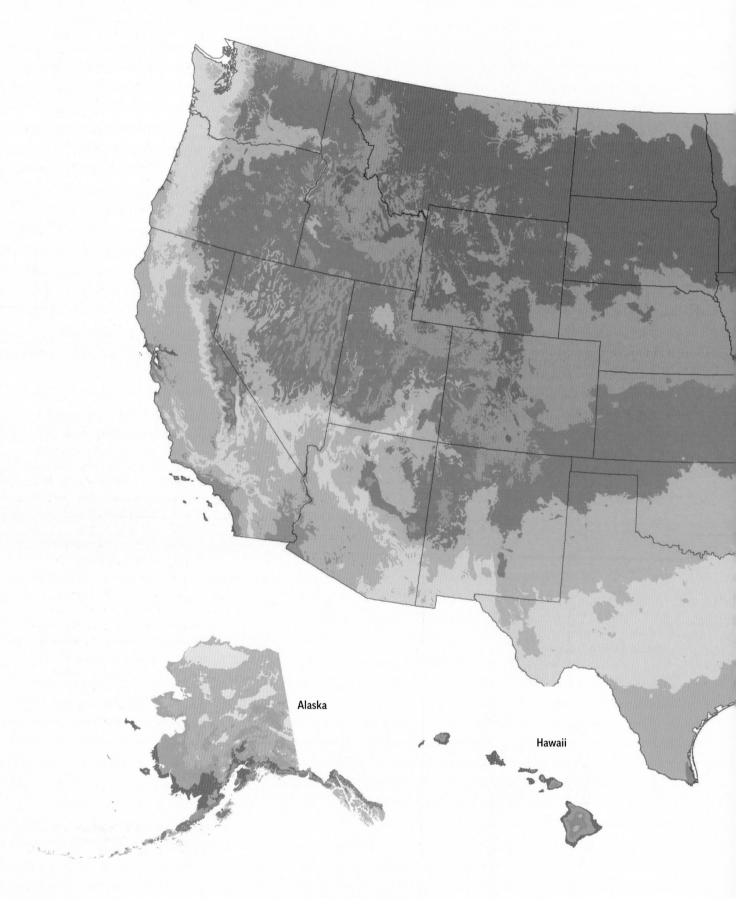

Alaska

Hawaii

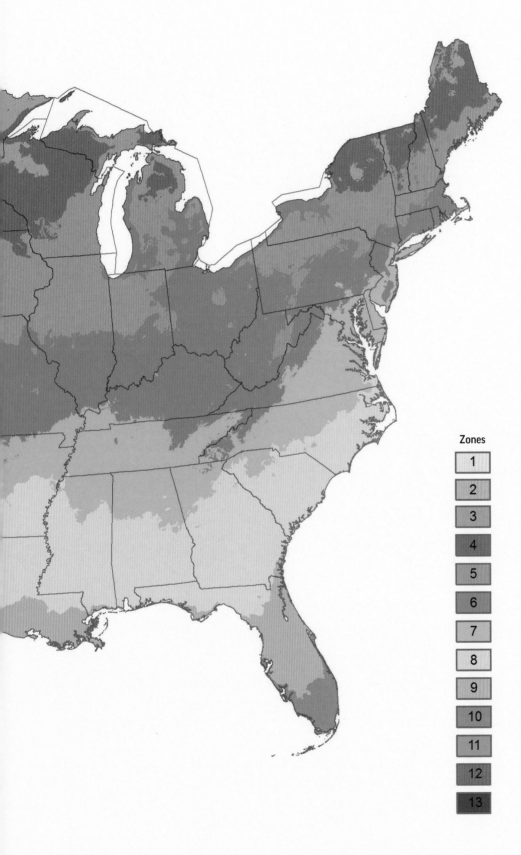

The most recent plant hardiness zone map of the United States is based on temperatures recorded between 1976 and 2005, and uses an algorithm to estimate climates in previously unrecorded areas, allowing for a more thorough and accurate set of data than previous models. USDA has officially adopted this map, and has published it online as a region-specific, interactive resource for gardeners and agriculturalists.

To determine which zone your garden falls within, and for more information on plant hardiness zones across the United States, you can visit the USDA website: planthardiness.ars.usda.gov. However, research indicates that further changes to US temperatures and hardiness zones are projected over the coming decades, as temperatures rise nationally.

Most species will be unaffected by changing climates in the short term, although if considering lanting trees with a particularly long lifespan, it's worth making sure that it's a variety likely to withstand the changing temperatures. Based on the previous data, which suggests a continuing pattern towards warmer growing regions heading north, this is especially pertinent to those based in a region just north of the cusp of a hardiness zone.

Cities and communities are preparing for the impacts of climate change in the coming decades. Some of the impacts predicted are warmer winter temperatures, changes in precipitation patterns, increased storm activity and wind velocity and more extreme events, such as drought and heavy rainfall.

Zones

1
2
3
4
5
6
7
8
9
10
11
12
13

Map courtesy of USDA Agricultural Research Service. Mapping by PRISM Climate Group, Oregon State University, 2012.

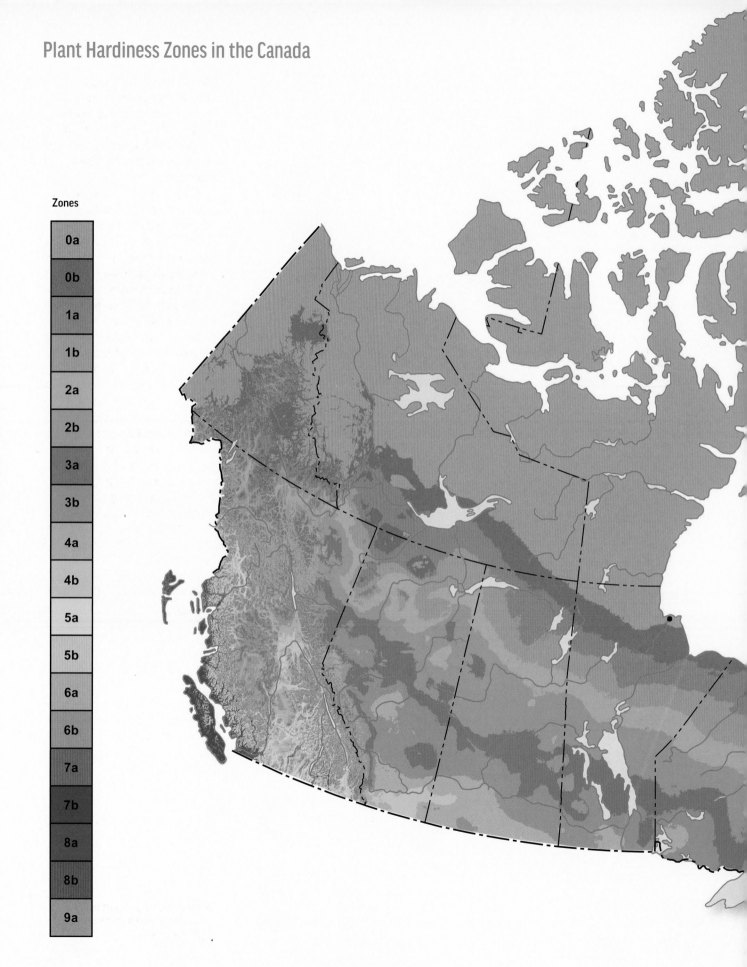

Zones

0a
0b
1a
1b
2a
2b
3a
3b
4a
4b
5a
5b
6a
6b
7a
7b
8a
8b
9a

TREE SELECTION AND PLACEMENT

Canadian plant hardiness zones were devised using a method similar the US maps, but they take into account more region-specific variables, such as average frost-free periods, rainfall, and maximum snow depths.

For more information about plant hardiness zones in Canada, including interactive maps of your province or territory, you can visit the Natural Resources Canada website: www.planthardiness.gc.ca.

When considering planting trees with a particularly long lifespan, it's worth making sure that it's a variety likely to withstand the changing temperatures. Based on the previous hardiness zone data, this is especially pertinent to those based in a region immediately north of the cusp of a warmer zone, and particu-larly in the western provinces.

Most species of trees will be unaffected by changing climates in the short term, although gardeners with a more long-range view would do well to chose their varieties accordingly.

There are endless shades of green!

are more tolerant than others, but all trees react to rainfall, humidity and temperature conditions. For example, a tree native to Zone 6 may survive in warmer regions of Zone 5 until low temperatures cause fatal freezing damage; whereas trees native to Zone 5 will likely be able to withstand colder conditions.

Important Factors to Consider When Selecting a Tree

In order to choose the right tree, you have to know what you want.

- What is the purpose or desired effect?
- What tree types are native to your area? What trees are available at your local garden center?
- What trees are best suited to your location?

Do you have the space for the tree? Picture the tree when it is mature or fully grown. Will it interfere with anything? Planting a tree too close to another tree is a very common error. The tree may be small when planted, but as it matures it can crowd out other trees, resulting in the trees struggling as they compete for space, light and nutrients. A tree planted too close to a building can also cause a lot of problems. The tree may have to be severely pruned to clear branches from the structure or removed completely because of interference with the building. Roots may also block underground pipes. The key to avoiding these situations is to know how big the tree you buy will get when it reaches maturity. Ideally, you should plant a tree that can reach its natural size in a spot where it is going to have lots of room to grow and not interfere with anything around it. Allow sufficient space to accommodate mature size. If the space is not sufficient, choose a smaller tree.

Is the tree hardy enough for your area? Know your hardiness zone. Trees and shrubs will be healthiest and look most attractive when provided with their preferred growing conditions.

Consider the drainage of the planting location, which is a very important but often overlooked factor in choosing a tree. Does the water drain well or does it pool and sit on top of the ground, leaving the area wet? Trees planted in a site that is too wet or too dry will often die in the first year.

Consider the soil type in your area. Certain trees require specific soil conditions. Drainage is poor in a heavy clay soil, while a soil that is too sandy will lack in nutrients. Also, if the soil is compacted, the growth of the tree will be reduced because of lack of oxygen in the root zone.

When purchasing a tree for your garden, consider the many characteristics that trees offer, such as interesting bark, shape and size, fruit seeds, flowers and cones, leaf and needle formation, shade and color. Tree options range from evergreens that keep their foliage throughout the winter to deciduous trees that bear fruit and nuts and shed their leaves in the fall before becoming **dormant** in the winter.

Trees of Interesting Shapes

- Pyramidal trees such as pyramidal oaks, spruces and firs
- Weeping trees, from the dramatic golden weeping willow to the smaller weeping mulberry
- Multiple-trunk trees such as birch clumps, serviceberries and amur maples

Trees come in many shapes and sizes. Choose carefully so that the tree meets your needs. Recognizing tree shapes helps in identification, as many trees have a characteristic shape. Consider, for example, the classic vase shape of the American elm.

Pyramidal

Columnar

Multi-stemmed

Full-crowned

Fountain

Vase-shaped

Weeping

Spreading

Tree Characteristics

There are many characteristics to consider when choosing a tree for your space, including:

- interesting bark;
- different types of fruit seeds, flowers and cones;
- comfortable shade, either to relax under or to help moderate the temperature of your home, keeping it cool in summer;
- sizes and shape — for example, columnar trees grow very narrow and

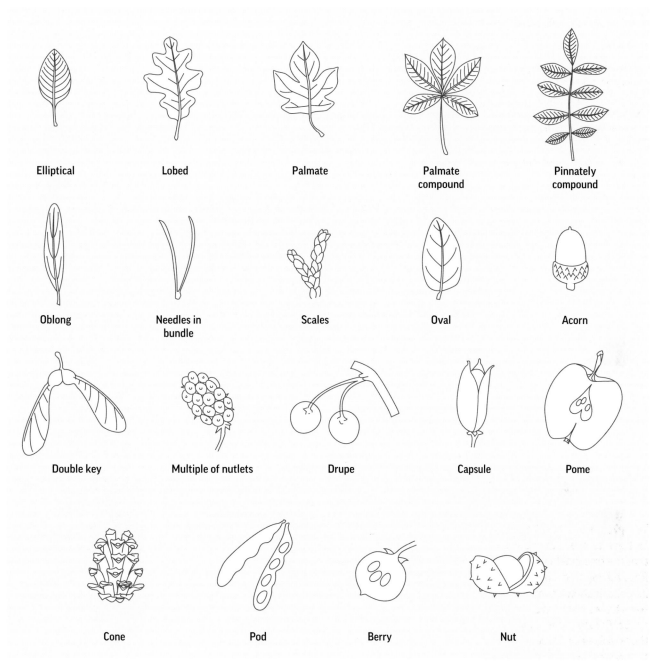

Elliptical   Lobed   Palmate   Palmate compound   Pinnately compound

Oblong   Needles in bundle   Scales   Oval   Acorn

Double key   Multiple of nutlets   Drupe   Capsule   Pome

Cone   Pod   Berry   Nut

upright, and many trees have sculptural forms and shapes visible in the winter that offer interest during the long cold season;

- inspiring color — consider a blue spruce with its beautiful blue or a crimson king maple with its dark purple leaves;
- leaf color and shape — the tulip tree has a delightful leaf, as does the mulberry, which can have two or three different-shaped leaves on the same branch; the compound leaves of the Kentucky coffee tree or the black walnut are pleasing, and ginkgo leaves are fan shaped;
- appeal to wildlife — coniferous trees, for example, provide excellent shelter for wildlife;

Leaf shapes and sizes provide interest in the landscape. Fruits and cones can attract wildlife and offer variety, and may remain on branches in the winter, providing winter enjoyment. Leaves, fruits and cones are all identification features.

Tree and Shrub Suitability Guide

Trees That Are Suitable for Sandy Soil

- Norway maple
- Silver maple
- Hackberry
- Linden
- Honey locust
- Catalpa
- Red pine
- Jack pine
- Colorado spruce
- Siberian elm
- Staghorn sumac

Trees That Are Suitable for Wet Soil

- Red maple
- Willow
- White oak
- Pin oak
- Cedar
- Larch
- Basswood
- Silver maple
- European ash
- Poplar
- River birch
- Holly

Trees with Interesting Bark

- White birch
- London plan
- Paperbark maple
- Scotch pine
- Blue beech
- American beech
- River birch
- Hop tree

Flowering Trees

- Magnolia
- Crab apple
- Eastern redbud
- Flowering dogwood
- Ornamental pear
- Serviceberry
- Japanese tree lilac
- Witch hazel
- Hawthorn
- Japanese flowering cherry
- Golden chain
- Red buckeye

Shade or Large Trees

- Tulip tree
- Oak (red, white, burr, etc.)
- White pine
- Ginkgo
- Little-leaf linden
- Dawn redwood (deciduous evergreen)
- Sugar maple
- Kentucky coffee tree
- Katsura tree

- Red maple
- Black walnut
- Black locust
- Sassafras
- Sweet gum
- Tamarack
- Cucumber tree

Low-Maintenance Trees and Shrubs

Some plants are more low maintenance than others. These trees are adaptable and hardy, and do not need much pruning, fertilizing or additional watering:

- Box elder
- Leyland cypress
- Forsythia
- Hackberry
- Hawthorn
- Juniper
- Thornless honey locust
- Amur maple
- Hedge maple
- Redbud
- Shadblow (serviceberry)
- Japanese zelkova

Multiseason Stars

These trees offer good foliage in spring and summer, and throughout the fall:

- Japanese maple (strong fall color)
- Apple serviceberry (white flowers in spring)

- Flowering dogwood (spectacular flowers in spring)
- Winter King green hawthorn (lustrous green leaves in summer)
- Flowering crab apple (covered with flowers in spring)
- Sargent cherry (good fall color)
- Chinese quince (attractive fruit in summer)
- Sassafras (neon fall color)

"Messy" Trees and Shrubs

Some trees are known for the messy debris they drop in your yard. They include:

- Crab apple (lots of small fruit)
- Catalpa (long, leathery seedpods)
- Black cherry (messy fruit)
- Gingko (females' stinky fruit)
- Mimosa (seedpods)
- Mulberry (messy fruit that leaves stains)
- Eastern poplar (messy fruit)
- Pin oak (lots of acorns)
- Plane tree (generally messy leaves, twigs and fruit)
- Black walnut (nut husks that stain black when opened or damaged)
- Weeping willow (lots of small leaves and branches)

- delicious fruit, such as pears, cherries, apples, etc.;
- flowers, from the stunning saucer magnolia to the small yellow flower of the witch hazel, which can last well into the winter;
- deciduous tree leaves, which change and die, and may remain on the tree well into the winter season (examples are the pyramidal English oak and the pin oak); and
- branching patterns, such as the zigzag growth of the honey locust tree or the upright spreading growth of the zelkova tree.

  Above are listed a few examples of tree types with specific characteristics to help you consider the options available. Bear in mind that there are

Invasive Trees and Shrubs

Some trees and shrubs crowd out other desirable plants. They include:

- Japanese barberry
- Scotch broom
- Buckthorn
- Bush honeysuckle
- Black locust
- Paper mulberry
- Autumn olive
- Siberian elm
- Tamarisk
- Tree of heaven

Good for Screening

These trees and shrubs make good screens and provide privacy without the extra work of clipping or shearing for formality:

- Abelia
- Leyland cypress
- Evergreen euonymus
- Forsythia
- Holly
- Box honeysuckle
- Juniper
- Hedge maple
- Oleander
- Yew

Beds and Borders

When combining trees and shrubs with perennial flowers in your garden (mixed bed or border), consider small trees such as:

- Red buckeye
- Dwarf conifer
- Japanese maple
- Paperbark maple
- Crape myrtle
- Serviceberry
- Carolina silver bell

And shrubs such as:

- Azalea
- Boxwood
- Butterfly bush
- Clethra
- Holly
- Japanese kerria
- California lilac

Trees and Shrubs for Shady Places

These trees offer full shade:

- Japanese holly
- Mountain laurel
- Rhododendron
- Hemlock
- Maple-leaf viburnum
- Wayfaring tree
- Yellowroot

These trees offer partial shade:

- Japanese maple
- Serviceberry
- Sweet azalea
- Redbud
- Smooth hydrangea
- Sweet bay
- Royal azalea

These trees offer dappled or light shade:

- Red chokeberry
- Dogwood
- Witch hazel
- Spicebush
- Andromeda
- Yew

Deciduous Salt-Tolerant Trees

- Amur maple
- Horse chestnut
- Yellow birch
- Persimmon
- White ash
- Black walnut
- Sweet gum
- Mulberry
- London plane tree
- Poplar
- Sargent cherry
- White oak
- Red oak
- Black locust
- Japanese tree lilac
- Bald cypress

Evergreen Salt-Tolerant Trees

- Chinese juniper
- Eastern red cedar
- Southern magnolia
- Live oak
- Colorado spruce
- Swiss mountain pine
- Arborvitae

Pollution-Tolerant Landscape Trees and Shrubs

- Hedge maple
- Hackberry
- Hawthorn
- Gingko
- Crape myrtle
- Magnolia
- Amur cork tree
- Japanese black pine
- Douglas fir
- English oak
- Sumac
- Chinese scholar tree
- Little-leaf linden

Intolerant Landscape Trees

- Sugar maple
- Red maple
- Serviceberry
- Catalpa
- Larch
- White pine
- Quaking aspen
- Willow
- American elm

literally hundreds of species to choose from, so you may want to consult the many informative gardening magazines and books that feature trees in different regions. It is worth reviewing publications with comprehensive lists and details, such as *The Encyclopedia of Trees: Canada and the United States* by Sam Benvie, Lois Hole's *Favorite Trees and Shrubs*, Ortho's *All About Trees* and *Sunset Trees and Shrubs*.

When choosing a tree, decide what characteristics you find attractive and what purpose you have in mind. Take a walk around your neighborhood and see what kinds of trees have been planted. Visit a tree nursery, look at the selection of trees and ask questions of the nursery staff.

Instead of a fence, consider planting a row of trees for privacy.

You may be inspired by what you see planted in neighboring properties and decide to buy a certain tree, but not know what kind of tree it is. One option is to ask the owner if you may take a small twig sample using your gardening **secateurs**, which you could then take to your local nursery or garden center. Knowledgeable staff should be able to inform you of its species type. You can also identify trees yourself with the help of a good reference book. Leaves are often the most identifiable features on a tree — but in the winter you will have to examine other parts instead. Look at the tree's overall structure, the type of bark and buds, and any seeds or fruit on the tree. Most plant reference books have a series of keys that you can follow to determine tree species. Just follow the keys, using all of the features you observed.

Planning and Design

Take a careful look at your space and think about the following points when you are selecting trees and considering where to place them:

- **Purpose:** Do you want to feature trees in your garden for privacy? Do you want a tree that will produce flowers for cutting? Do you want a companion piece to the architecture of your house? A natural element in a crowded urban area? A property line or barrier? A specimen or accent plant?

- **Theme:** Is there a particular type of garden you want to create, such as a lush Victorian setting or a spare modern landscape?
- **Maintenance:** How much time do you have to tend to your trees?
- **Continuity:** Do your plans complement the area surrounding your garden space?
- **Location:** Seriously consider where you are going to plant your trees, because transplanting trees and shrubs causes them stress.
- **Placement:** As a general rule, install plants from largest to smallest (placing the smallest at the front).
- **Root competition and shade:** You must acknowledge a tree's natural dominance when choosing other plants to grow around it.
- **Cost:** How much do you want to spend?
- **Appearance:** Envision the tree's appearance in all seasons.
- **Disease Prevention:** Consider the plant's susceptibility to pests or disease. For example, the European white birch is a poor choice if you live east of the Rocky Mountains (where the bronze birch borer, a pest that can cause the death of valuable trees, zeroes in), but a good choice for the western states (where the pest is absent).
- **Windbreaks:** Windbreaks reduce wind, noise and soil erosion, and they help to retain moisture by collecting snow and creating a milder **microclimate** for nearby plants. Study where windbreaks should be planted to ensure the greatest amount of protection for plants and buildings.

Review these special concerns for particular sites:

- Watch out for overhead or underground utility lines, septic tanks or other physical constraints.
- Call city hall and/or the electric company about curbside or street trees, as they may have lists of trees that are recommended or not permitted. The ideal street trees are short, neat, carefree and tough, with strong limbs that don't fall off.
- Consider planting small, slender trees with fragrant flowers, berries that attract birds, fancy foliage or interesting bark next to a patio or deck.
- If you have the space, the lawn is the best place for a large tree. Make sure the tree has an open canopy that doesn't cast too much shade and roots that never appear at the surface. You should also ensure the tree will adapt to the same watering and fertilizing practices that you use for the lawn.
- For a screening effect you need height and density, not width, so look for narrow, upright tree varieties. Tall, skinny trees that keep their lower limbs are uncommon, but can be special-ordered from a local garden center.

Trees soften the harsh aspects of brick and concrete buildings in the city. In most sophisticated cities — including London and Paris — they form part of the urban architecture. Hugely transformative and not just plants, trees are elements of the landscape used to define space and to separate and connect it. They are an indispensable aspect of the urban fabric, just as important as sidewalks, roads or buildings.

After deciduous trees have dropped their leaves for the winter, evergreens continue to provide interest.

Planting for Landscape Enhancement and Functionality

- Within every yard there are microclimates, areas that may be either warmer or colder than surrounding areas. On a fall morning after a freezing night, you will sometimes notice that frost has hit only certain exposed spots of your yard. Trees help produce microclimates. The warmest parts of your garden will be near tall trees or large shrubs, hedges, fences and walls. Such obstructions trap heat and provide shelter from the wind. Select protected spots for tender plant varieties and reserve exposed areas for hardier plants.

- Newly planted evergreens and non-hardy specimens should be planted in locations that cause them the least stress — ideally, sites that are sunny in summer and shaded in winter.

- Tender evergreens like rhododendrons are most susceptible to foliage damage.

- Rather than choosing a tree that will grow too large for its site, pick a named cultivar of the chosen species with a small growth habit or with dwarf or weeping characteristics.

- By choosing a variety of trees, you add diversity to the area, which strengthens the ecology of the region, nurturing wildlife and promoting healthy plants that are more tolerant of disease, pests and drought.

- Deciduous versus evergreen: Most deciduous trees start their growth in spring with a burst of new leaves or flowers and last throughout the summer in full foliage. Leaf color often changes in the fall before the leaves drop. Winter can reveal a fascinating structure of bare limbs. Broad-leafed evergreens are not generally able to survive in extremely cold-winter climates. Needle-leafed evergreens include those with actual needles — pines, firs and spruce — as well as junipers and cypresses, whose leaves are merely tiny scales. All evergreens keep their uniform appearance all year long, though they lose some foliage every year.

- Strive for harmony and scale within your garden to create enduring beauty. Your trees will be celebrated for generations to come.

What Makes a Tree Suitable for the City?

Urban communities are beautifully suited to tree plantings, because trees help to decrease air and noise pollution and can make city streets look more natural. However, city life creates challenges for homeowners, so consider the following points when selecting a tree for your space:

- Select a hardy tree that is able to tolerate road salt used in winter and air pollution, such as emissions from cars and trucks. Choose a tree that is resistant to insect and disease problems so you can avoid the use of **chemical pesticides**.

Opt for a cultivar or dwarf species if you have limited space for a tree.

Trees Can Create Work

Bear in mind the amount of litter certain trees can create. Flowers and fruit will fall from trees and need to be cleaned up. Fruit will rot if it is left on the ground and will also attract insects such as bees or wasps. Fast-growing trees, such as the willow or poplar, tend to have weak wood and can drop small twigs and branches, especially during windy conditions. In some years, trees will produce an abundance of seeds, while cones from evergreen trees can cause quite a mess.

Smaller tree varieties work well in landscaped settings.

- If the tree can tolerate drought conditions, it can survive in harsh urban conditions.
- Crab apple and mountain ash trees provide beautiful flowers in the spring. Weak-wooded trees, such as willows, poplars and silver maples, usually drop small twigs or branches, while flowering trees will drop their petals. Can you tolerate such messes?
- A tree that provides shade may be highly prized; nevertheless, heavy shade will result in a poor lawn.

Common complaints about street trees include:

- messiness (crab apple, mountain ash);
- too much foliage/shade: grass does not grow, sap or waste from insects drips on cars or driveways, causing damage (Norway maple);
- roots from trees heave or crack driveways, walkways or foundations (silver maple);
- branches obstruct view of traffic on road when backing out of driveway (spruce, cedar, juniper);
- street trees interfere with residents' private trees and impede their growth; and
- street trees block or restrict light from a streetlight.

Urban gardeners should select tree specimens that won't outgrow their space. Decorative small-sized trees include eastern redbud, pagoda dogwood, Japanese tree lilac, serviceberry and paperbark maple.

Take a Walk

Walk around your neighborhood and see what kinds of trees appear to be thriving. If you have difficulty identifying a tree, ask the owner's permission to take a small twig or leaf sample then bring it to your local garden center or refer to a tree reference book with keys you can follow to determine tree species.

As you begin to familiarize yourself with a wide variety of trees, take note of how a tree looks during different seasons. Pick out certain features that will help you recognize the tree throughout the year, without leaves for example. Observe the shape, structure, bark, fruit and flowers as they present themselves at various times of the year.

One good identifying feature to look for is the tree's buds, which can be very distinctive. You won't forget the large sticky buds of the horse chestnut tree or the long, pointed cigar-shaped buds of the beech tree. Upon closer examination, you will notice that tree buds are usually opposite or alternately placed on the twig. Knowing if the buds are opposite or alternate will narrow your list of possibilities. Get to know your buds using a good tree identification book and enjoy discovering the wide variety of trees in the landscape.

Strategically planted trees camouflage unsightly items like exterior cooling units.

Evergreens planted on the north side of a house can lower winter heating costs by up to 10 percent.

How to Maintain Your Street Tree

Municipalities throughout North America encourage residents to plant trees to help decrease pollution. In addition, many local governments plant trees along city streets, and employ arborists and forestry workers to maintain them. Often, homeowners can even choose the type of tree they would like featured on their street. If you have a city tree on your lot, consider the following tips to help maintain its health:

- Avoid damaging the trunk with weed eaters and lawn mowers. Damage to the bark can kill the tree.
- Do not mound soil or grass clippings around the trunk of the tree.
- If you maintain a healthy lawn and boulevard, a mature tree will usually receive sufficient water. However, it is advisable to supply water to the tree in excessively dry periods. Also, newly planted trees need plenty of water. Because it is difficult for municipalities to water these trees on a regular basis, you may want to take on this job.
- Contact your municipality to have the tree pruned to remove low, **interfering limbs**. General pruning will also benefit the overall health of the tree.

Dig your hole wide and deep enough so there is room for the roots to expand and grow once they are released from the burlap or wire basket from which the tree came.

Maintain your city street tree by avoiding damage inflicted by weed eaters and lawn mowers, and by watering when necessary.

- Avoid planting flowers under the tree or piling rocks against the trunk of the tree.
- A wood-chip **mulch** of 3 to 4 inches around the base of the tree (but not against the trunk) will help to retain moisture, moderate soil temperature and reduce weed growth.

Shade trees have a considerable impact on cooling your home and decreasing energy costs. If you plant a deciduous tree on the west and south sides of your home you may reduce your air-conditioning needs by up to 40 percent. You can decrease winter heating costs by up to 10 percent by planting evergreens on the north side of your home to act as a windbreak.

Tree-Planting Incentives

If you're lucky enough to own a large property, check with your local conservation authority or government agencies to see if they provide tree seedlings or whips to plant on your property. There may also be incentives for planting trees on your property. You will benefit your area and the environment by planting trees in large quantities.

Trees can be grown for lumber or for fine wood for furniture, among other purposes. Black walnut is particularly valued for its wood for furniture. Cherry wood is sought after for fine furniture. Mature trees of these species can be worth a lot of money. Sugar maples can be grown and tapped for their sap, which is made into maple syrup.

Fall versus Spring Planting

- Experienced gardeners know that fall is an ideal time to plant new trees. In the fall, it is easy to see where the tree fits in because of the lack of full foliage. Also, cool weather is less stressful to trees than hot, dry summer weather. Shrubs, trees and evergreens will be noticeably advanced with regard to growth and bloom compared to those planted next spring. The younger feeder roots of trees planted in the fall provide the necessary water and nutrients for the plant to become established, resulting in substantial new growth as soon as the soil begins to warm at the start of a new planting season.

- Spring is a peak time for selection and choice. It is the best time to plant trees that are not locally grown because it allows them time to adjust to new climate conditions. Trees still have plenty of time to set their roots before the stress of summer heat.

easily. Sandy soil is well-drained and well-aerated, but needs frequent water and nutrient applications to maintain adequate moisture and fertility.

The best soils contain a mixture of particle sizes and shapes, balancing clay's nutrient-holding capacity with sand's permeability. Fortunately, most soils fall somewhere between the extremes of clay and sand, and need little special treatment to grow trees and shrubs well.

Nevertheless, the following soil conditions usually require special treatment:

- **Compact soil:** In new housing developments, the soil will have been compressed by heavy equipment during construction. Such soil drains poorly, is difficult to dig and is nearly impossible for roots to penetrate. Special soil-loosening equipment may remedy the situation; contact an **arborist** for more information. An alternative is to construct raised beds and fill them with good soil.

- **Shallow soil:** A shallow layer of good soil may be found on new home sites where the developer has spread new soil over the soil compacted during construction. Shallow soil may also occur naturally over a layer of dense hardpan; in the Southwest, gardeners must cope with an alkaline hardpan known as **caliche**. If a hardpan layer is thin, you may be able to dig full-width planting holes through it to more porous soil beneath. You could also consider planting a little higher, as you would for clay soil. Add soil and mulch to the top of the root ball (but don't bury it).

- **Acid or alkaline soil:** You may be able to moderate chemical extremes with soil treatments available from nurseries, but you'll need to repeat treatment, depending on the result you require. Amending soil to optimum conditions is difficult to achieve and results are not permanent. You'll have to apply the treatment regularly.

To determine the type of soil in your garden, pick up a handful of moist soil and squeeze it.

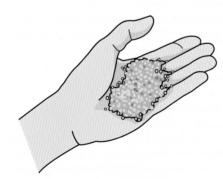

Sandy soil – can barely be contained in your hand and feels gritty and non-sticky

Clay soil – can form into a ball, feels smooth and sticks together

Loam soil – the ideal soil holds together when squeezed, feels most and spongy, and crumbles easily

There is a far simpler approach than amending soil. Simply choose trees that will thrive in the normal acidity or alkalinity of your soil. Your soil is one of three types: acid, alkaline or neutral.

This characteristic is measured in **pH**, with a pH of 7 representing neutral. Readings of less than 7 indicate acid soil, readings higher than 7 indicate alkaline soil. If readings are extreme in either direction, key nutrients are bound up tightly in compounds in the soil and not available to roots. Most trees and shrubs will prosper in soils registering a pH of 5.5 to 6.5. A soil test will confirm your pH level. Soil test kits sold at nurseries will give you ballpark readings, but professional tests will provide more precise results.

When to plant

The best time of year to plant depends on your climate and the type of tree you are planting. In general, planting should be done in the spring (March through May) and the fall (October through November), because increased soil moisture and moderate temperatures are favorable conditions for planting. Aim to plant the tree early enough in the spring or fall to allow the roots to grow and establish before the harsher conditions of summer or winter arrive. Certain trees are better planted in the spring, so they have more time to get established. Consult local nursery staff about the appropriate time to plant a specific tree.

In the southern U.S., planting can also take place during the winter months. Summer planting is never recommended, because heat and drought are especially stressful to newly planted trees. In milder regions, where the soil seldom freezes, you can plant trees and shrubs throughout the year, though fall through winter is the preferred period. In colder regions, planting in late winter to early spring will get most trees off to the best start.

Some gardeners prefer to plant trees in the fall after dormancy sets in, but at least one month before the soil freezes. Cooler weather allows for greater comfort while digging, and trees and shrubs still have time to put their roots into the soil before temperatures drop. The young feeder roots of trees planted in the fall provide the necessary water and nutrients for plants to become established, resulting in substantial new growth as soon as the soil begins to warm through at the start of spring. Trees planted the previous fall will grow and bloom more quickly than trees newly planted in spring.

When spring planting, ensure maximum first-year growth with the least stress on a new plant by planting in advance of the growing season, while the soil is cool. This will give the tree's roots a chance to grow into the new soil before foliage growth begins, which places demands on the root system.

- **Balled and burlapped trees** are available to be planted from early autumn and springtime. Remember, the root ball must not dry out.
- **Bare-root trees** are available only during autumn and winter, when they

The Advantages of Fall Planting

With the fall's cooling air, still-warm soil holds heat from the summer and roots can begin to grow. Winter's precipitation provides plenty of moisture for the soil. Although the soil is cold, roots continue to grow slowly using the plant's stored food. Warming air and sunshine during the spring provide for top growth and the continued growth of roots. By late spring, trees planted in the fall experience a growth surge.

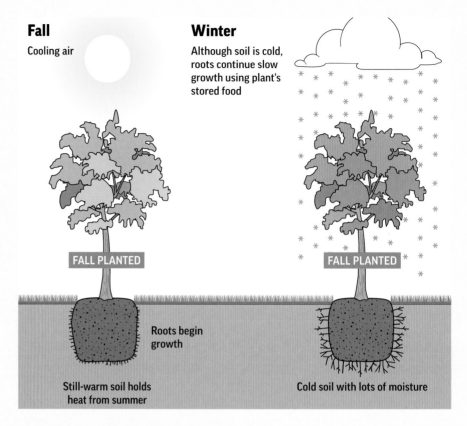

Fall

Cooling air

FALL PLANTED

Roots begin growth

Still-warm soil holds heat from summer

Winter

Although soil is cold, roots continue slow growth using plant's stored food

FALL PLANTED

Cold soil with lots of moisture

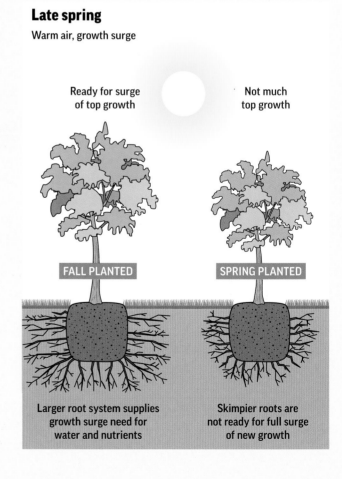

Early spring

Warming air

Top growth beginning on both plants

FALL PLANTED

SPRING PLANTED

Cold soil

Root growth continues

Roots start slowly

Late spring

Warm air, growth surge

Ready for surge of top growth

Not much top growth

FALL PLANTED

SPRING PLANTED

Larger root system supplies growth surge need for water and nutrients

Skimpier roots are not ready for full surge of new growth

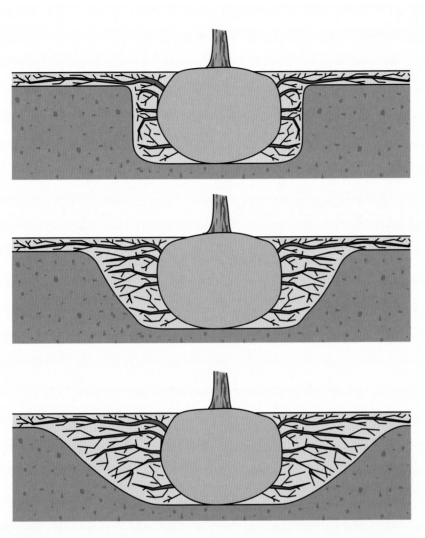

Use your shovel to gauge the depth of your hole. Place the shovel in the hole and check the level of the desired planting depth with your finger on the handle of the shovel, then match that depth to the tree's root ball to get the approximate depth of the hole.

A properly dug planting hole provides roots with optimal growing conditions. A broad planting hole (bottom), two to three times the size of the root ball, is ideal.

are dormant. Their roots, which must be kept moist before planting, are buried in a moisture-retentive medium.

- **Container-grown trees** are available whenever the ground is not frozen. They are best planted in cooler months, but may be set during spring or summer if you water adequately during dry periods and shelter the tree from intense sun and wind.

How to dig a planting hole

- Call your local utility company before you dig to check for underground wires.
- When digging in poorly drained clay soil, avoid **glazing**, which occurs when the sides and bottom of the hole become smooth, forming a barrier through which water and roots may not pass. Glazing will

Forming a berm or dike around the outer edge of the root ball will help collect water, keeping the root area moist.

Balled-and-burlapped trees should always be lifted by the root ball, never by the trunk.

inhibit proper root development into the surrounding soil. Use a fork to roughen up the sides and bottom of the hole.

- The width of the hole should be two to three times the size of the root ball of the tree you are planting.
- The hole should be saucer-shaped, so the roots can spread horizontally near the surface, where optimum growth takes place.
- Planting depth is important. A common mistake is to plant the tree too deep. If you plant the tree too deep its roots won't be able to access enough oxygen to ensure proper growth. Also, if you dig too narrow a hole, the tree's root structure won't expand to nourish and anchor the tree. The tree should not look like a telephone pole going into the ground — that is, the trunk should have a flare to it and be wider at the bottom, tapering as it extends upward.
- Dig more deeply around the edges of the bottom of the hole. This leaves a slight mound of untouched soil that will support the plant at a proper depth and prevent the tree from settling and water from pooling.
- It is best to have the **root collar** 1 to 3 inches higher than ground level in case of possible settling. If possible, try to orient the tree in the same direction it was grown. Ask the staff at the tree farm in which direction it grew. Position the tree for best viewing and face the lowest branches away from the greatest pedestrian and vehicular traffic.

The preceding section addresses how to dig a basic planting hole for all types of trees, while the steps below address how to plant specific tree stock.

How to plant

BALLED AND BURLAPPED TREES
- The burlap should not be removed until your tree is positioned in the hole and is upright. This ensures that the roots are kept intact.
- Set your balled and burlapped tree in the planting hole, with its root ball resting on the mound of untouched soil.
- Untie the burlap and spread it out, uncovering half of the root ball. Gently cut loose the burlap without damaging the root ball. Also cut any rope away from the trunk.
- If there is a wire basket around the root ball, cut it so it will not impede the growth of the trunk and then trim away the top one-third of the wire basket. Make sure that no sharp pieces of the basket protrude through the soil.
- Leave the remaining burlap and/or wire under the root ball — roots grow out, not down.
- When the tree is positioned and straight, backfill the hole to just below the root collar, using the same soil that you dug out. Break up any large clumps and remove any debris. Amending the soil is not recommended, as roots tend to stay in pockets of amended soil instead of reaching out to become established. Lightly pack the backfill around the root ball.

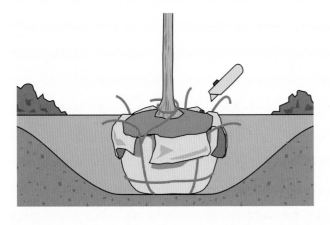

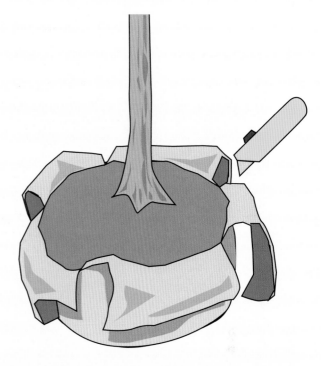

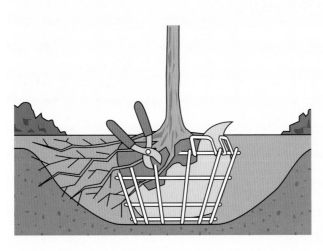

When the tree has been set in the hole at the proper depth and straightened, be sure to cut the rope from around the trunk and ball before you backfill the soil. Either peel back the burlap below ground level or cut it back so that none of the burlap is above the soil. If the ball is in a wire basket, cut back the top one-third of the basket.

- Once the hole is half full, pour a bit of water over the tree roots to help eliminate any air pockets that may be present. Continue to **backfill**, tamping the soil. (Do not pack the soil after you water.) Create a raised berm or dike around the root ball to help retain moisture around the roots.

These key planting steps are quick and easy to complete, but it is surprising how often they are forgotten. Many trees' root balls are girdled when rope is not removed from the trunk. This will kill the tree, as it makes water and nutrient uptake impossible. Any burlap left exposed above ground acts like a wick and dries out the root ball, killing roots that are vital for plant establishment. Be careful not to pile dirt against the tree trunk, as it can cause bark rot.

Balled and burlapped trees are best planted as soon as possible after delivery, but they can be stored for a few weeks in a shady area as long as the root ball is moist. Balled and burlapped trees are generally larger than container trees and can weigh hundreds of pounds.

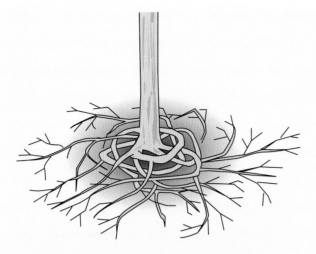

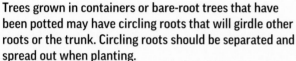

Trees grown in containers or bare-root trees that have been potted may have circling roots that will girdle other roots or the trunk. Circling roots should be separated and spread out when planting.

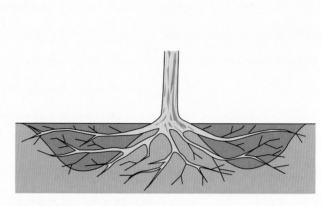

Bare-root trees should be planted on a compacted soil mound. Spread the roots out over the mound, keeping them from crossing and becoming tangled.

BARE-ROOT TREES

- Build a cone of earth in the center of the hole, around which to spread the roots. Spread roots over the cone, placing your plant at the same depth (or a bit higher) as it was in the growing field.
- Add backfill soil nearly to the top of the hole, tamping it as you fill. Add water. If the plant settles, move it up and down in the saturated soil to raise it to the proper level.

Plant bare-root trees during the dormant season, before roots and buds begin to grow. Plant the tree as soon as possible after delivery. If you cannot plant it immediately, store the tree in a cool area with moist packing around the roots until you're ready to plant it — the sooner the better.

CONTAINER PLANTS

- The roots of container plants may be coiled or matted. Remove the tree from the container and remove the soil from the outer few inches of the root ball. Then, uncoil any circling or twisted roots with your fingers or a blunt instrument.
- Lightly break up the soil around the sides of the planting zone to allow roots that spread quickly to easily extend and grow outward as they anchor into the existing soil conditions.
- Spread the roots out over the mound of soil in the center of the hole. The top of the root ball should be approximately 2 inches above surrounding soil.
- Add backfill soil.

Container trees are usually sold in plastic or natural fiber pots. Although they are easy to handle and plant, their roots can become pot-bound or circling, which can inhibit root growth. Roots can also become girdled or be choked out by other circling roots. Be sure to check the root structure before purchasing a container tree. A container plant can be stored in a shady area for a brief period as long as the soil in the container is kept moist.

Before planting, slide the tree out of the container and gently score the sides with a knife to encourage rooting. Trees that come in natural fiber pots can be left in the pots when planted, but you should cut the top portion of the pot away to ensure that no part of it is exposed above soil level. Remove metal or plastic containers completely.

PLANTING TREES IN ABOVEGROUND CONTAINERS

Trees planted in aboveground containers have a difficult time surviving and are unlikely to live very long due to the following reasons:

- Containers hold only small amounts of soil.
- Roots cannot tolerate extreme changes in temperature. While soil temperature is relatively stable belowground, tree roots in aboveground containers bake in the summer and freeze in the winter. However, insulated containers are better able to withstand extreme temperatures than non-insulated ones.
- Soil in aboveground containers can dry out quickly, so container trees must be watered regularly. They cannot survive on rainfall alone.
- Often, containers do not provide adequate drainage. If its roots become waterlogged a tree can drown. Make sure your containers have drainage holes.

When planting container stock, remove the container and correct any circling roots. Spray the outer few inches of the root ball with water to aid in correcting circling roots. Spread the roots over the compacted mound and backfill. Create a berm to water.

To help increase the life of a tree planted in an aboveground container, make sure the container is insulated and that there is adequate drainage.

If you want to plant in aboveground containers, choose small trees with small root systems. You may need to replace aboveground trees every two to five years.

Care after Planting

Since trees are such a visible part of the landscape, care must be taken to ensure that proper growth conditions are maintained. Trees lose 70 to 95 percent of their root mass when transplanted. It usually takes transplanted trees one year for every inch of trunk diameter to regenerate their root mass.

Pruning at the time of planting is not recommended and should be limited to deadwood, broken branches and damaged limbs. **Corrective pruning** activity — such as pruning interfering limbs, poorly spaced limbs

This young tree is supported by two stakes and loosely tied burlap. It is also aided by a slow-release water bag, which helps the roots grow into the ground.

Live Long and Prosper

Help ensure that your trees enjoy a long life by completing the following maintenance tasks:

- **Stake only when necessary:** Most newly planted trees do not need to be staked. However, if you're planting in an open, windy area, staking a young tree provides it with support until its root system is established in the new location.
- **Mulch:** Use only organic mulch, such as wood chips or bark chips.
- **Water:** Watering is imperative in order for a tree's roots to grow into its surrounding soil. To test if your tree needs water, feel the soil 4 to 8 inches deep. If it is dry or only slightly damp, add water. Sandy soil will require more water than clay soil, which tends to hold moisture longer. Water the tree around the trunk. A slow trickle from a garden hose left to run over several hours is more beneficial than short, frequent watering, which promotes a shallow root system and makes the tree more vulnerable to environmental stress. Continue watering until mid-autumn, tapering off for lower temperatures that require less frequent watering. Give each of your trees one good long soak before freeze-up. Pay particular attention to evergreens, which lose moisture all winter because they don't shed their needles.
- **Fertilize:** Fertilizing may be necessary if your soil is deficient in essential macro- and micro-nutrients.

and weak crotches — should wait until the tree is established, after one or two growing seasons.

Watering

Proper watering practices are vital to the survival of your newly planted tree. Trees need soil moisture to encourage root growth and to supply water to leaves. Watering practices should suit the plant type and its environment, and must be appropriate for soil type and drainage. Young plants that are just getting established need more attention, as do mature specimens with extensive root systems.

Your soil type will also influence your watering schedule. Clay needs less frequent, but deeper, watering for the water to penetrate.

Every newly planted tree should be well watered at planting to eliminate air pockets and settle the tree firmly in place. Moisture should reach

Watering long and deep will benefit the growth and health of your tree.

12 inches below the soil surface to encourage ideal growth. Thereafter, water once or twice a week for the first few weeks until the root system becomes established. (Be careful not to overwater. Surprisingly, overwatering kills more trees than underwatering. Too much water will cause the leaves to turn yellow or fall off.)

Check the soil to determine when you need to water. You should water newly planted trees thoroughly when the top inch of soil has dried. For established trees, you may be able to wait until the top 2 to 4 inches of soil have lost moisture. You seldom need to water mature trees, except during periods of drought.

Prolonged rainfall will supply enough water to penetrate deeply. If you use sprinklers to duplicate rainfall, allow the water to soak into the soil over a period of time, which will provide the best penetration with the least waste through runoff and evaporation. You can use a soaker hose, too, a process known as "drip irrigation."

Continue watering until mid-autumn, tapering off as temperatures drop. In cold-winter regions, water trees well in advance of hard freezes. Give each of your trees one good long soaking before freeze-up. Plants that enter winter with dry soil have no moisture reserves in their needles to thwart drying winter winds. Evergreen plants are especially vulnerable to dry soil.

Staking

Staking is often used to re-establish young trees, especially bare-root stock. Some people believe that staking is not necessary and that trees will develop better if they are not staked. However, you might consider staking if your tree is planted in a very windy or exposed location.

Transplanted trees suffer from root loss, which limits a tree's ability to take in water and nutrients. Once a tree is planted, it will concentrate its energy on standing upright. To keep it straight and to keep it from being blown over, you may want to stake a young transplanted tree for a year or so.

Proper staking will also allow your tree enough room to move with the wind, which will enable it to develop a good trunk taper, which is important for stability. Staking will also help to reduce movement of the root ball, which may cause damage to new fine absorbing roots.

For best anchorage and to prevent damage, at least two stakes should be used for each tree. Stakes should be installed with the following tips in mind:

- Set stakes at equal distances from the trunk.
- Drive stakes into solid undisturbed ground at least 2 feet deep from the trunk to provide adequate stability for the tree and to avoid the root ball.
- Tie the tree to its stakes with suitable biodegradable material, like burlap. Avoid using wire encased in rubber hose, as it will prevent trunk expansion if it is left on too long.

- Leave at least 1 inch of space between each tie and the tree trunk. Remove stakes and ties after one year. If it is too dependent on supports, the trunk will not develop adequate strength.

If you decide to stake your tree, remember the following tips:

- Stake the tree only until it is able to stand on its own. If it is too dependent on supports, the trunk will not develop adequate strength.
- The staking material should not be too tight. Leave room for the tree to sway in the wind.
- The staking material should not be too loose. The tree should not rub against its stakes.
- Stakes should be buried at least 2 feet deep to provide ample support.
- Place your stakes carefully, so people won't trip over them.

If you decide your young tree should be staked, do so only for one year. Although you'll often see trees staked with wire and rubber, this is not a recommended practice. You should use a biodegradable material, like burlap, instead.

Trunk protection

You may choose to use a plastic tree guard around the trunk to minimize damage caused by mice, rabbits and other animals, and to protect it from mowers and string trimmers. (Wrapping is not recommended. This procedure, where a material such as burlap or crepe paper is wrapped around

A plastic tree guard offers young trees protection from mechanical injury and from mice and rabbits that may damage the trunk and bark.

the bark of young trees, fosters an environment for boring insects.) The guard should fit loosely and allow air to circulate around the trunk. You can also use plastic spirals to prevent mice, rabbits and deer from chewing the bark of young trees throughout the winter months.

Fertilizing

Trees growing in the wild get no fertilizer as we think of it. However, annual layers of fallen leaves and animal droppings decompose to release a small but continuous supply of nutrients. In the same way, many trees may grow successfully in yards and gardens without supplemental nutrients. If your tree displays significant new growth with good color each year, it is healthy and strong.

Urban trees, on the other hand, often grow in soil that does not contain sufficient nutrients for satisfactory growth. As trees and shrubs grow and develop, they require nutrients such as nitrogen, phosphorous and potassium. Topsoil is often removed during construction, and leaves and other plant parts are removed in gardening maintenance, robbing the soil of nutrients and organic matter. Consequently, most woody plants in urban areas benefit from the addition of fertilizer.

Fertilizing is not necessary if your tree appears to be healthy and strong — but, in some cases, fertilizing may be beneficial.

Plants can obtain nitrogen, phosphorous and potassium in a couple of different ways.

- Phosphorous and potassium must be present in the soil for it to be useful. Roots extract these two nutrients from films of water surrounding soil particles or from the particles themselves. The best time to apply **fertilizer** containing these two nutrients is before you plant, digging it well into the soil.
- Plants can obtain nitrogen from the air, from decaying matter in the soil and from fertilizer supplements. Much of the nitrogen that is found in soil is lost due to **leaching** or to its return to the atmosphere in a gaseous state. Removing leaf litter and other natural sources of nitrogen can disrupt the cycling of nitrogen in the soil.

A fertilizer containing all three of the above nutrients is called a **complete fertilizer** (5-10-5 nitrogen-phosphorus-potassium). Fertilizers are available in organic or inorganic forms. Inorganic fertilizers are quick releasing when dissolved in water, whereas organic fertilizers dissolve at a slower rate. Examples of natural organics are manures, sewage sludge, blood and bone meal.

When fertilizing trees, use fertilizers with slow-release or **controlled-release** nitrogen. To determine if a fertilizer is a slow-release one, look for the percentage of water-insoluble nitrogen on the label. If approximately half of the nitrogen is water-insoluble, it is considered slow-release.

In order for fertilizer to be absorbed by a tree's roots, its nutrients must be in solution, which requires soil moisture. This means that you must water the soil thoroughly after applying fertilizer so the nutrients are released.

ADVANTAGES OF FERTILIZING

- Fertilizers address nutrient deficiencies. Plants lacking in nitrogen display slow growth, small leaves and yellowing leaves (chlorosis). The application of fertilizer can often correct these problems.
- A tree that is growing vigorously is less susceptible to severe injury by certain diseases and insect pests.

DISADVANTAGES OF FERTILIZING

Heavy nitrogen fertilization promotes vegetative growth, or green leaf growth, which may delay flowering output. High rates of application in July and August will stimulate growth that won't harden off properly before the winter, which can result in winter-kill. Heavy nitrogen fertilization can also stimulate the activity of sap-sucking insects and certain diseases.

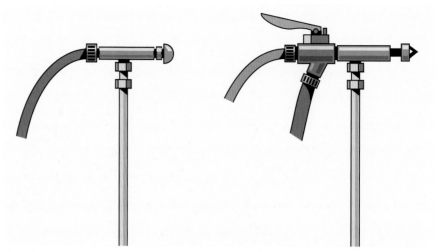

Used by homeowners, liquid root-feeding devices (left) are attached to a garden hose and have fertilizer cartridge chambers. Professional devices (right) use a spray tank under high pressure to deliver the fertilizer solution.

APPLICATION

Surface application with dry fertilizer is an easy and effective way to fertilize trees. Spread the necessary quantity of fertilizer uniformly over the root zone and then water slowly but thoroughly. The zone of actively absorbing roots begins well beyond the **drip line** of the tree and is approximately one-and-a-half to two times the crown radius.

To water and fertilize at the same time, apply fertilizer in a water suspension. In this process, the fertilizer solution is forced into the soil through a root feeder (a perforated, hollow rod attached to a water source). Attach a hose to the root feeder, insert fertilizer pellets or cartridges into the chamber at the top of the unit and then push the rod 12 inches into the soil, starting a few feet from the trunk and out beyond the drip line at 3-foot intervals. For best results, follow the manufacturer's instructions.

TIMING

Trees need nutrients when they are producing new growth. The best time to apply fertilizer is in late winter to early spring, depending on the climate. Fertilizer uptake in deciduous trees corresponds with the time of root growth, which, in general, starts before bud break and ends after leaf drop. Fall is also a good time to fertilize trees; many trees continue to grow roots in the fall after the shoots have stopped growing.

To prevent fertilizer runoff in the spring, do not apply it if the ground is frozen. During drought periods, roots will not readily absorb fertilizers. There is also additional risk of damage from salts.

In mild-winter regions with no frost, you can continue a fertilizer program throughout the summer. In cold-winter climates, discontinue fertilizer application in early summer. The new growth stimulated by later applications will be at risk when temperatures plummet. However, trees can benefit from one final application just before the first frost is expected.

Trees Are Self-Fertilizers

TREES IN NATURAL SETTINGS create their own mulch as they drop their leaves, twigs, fruit and flowers. This litter layer provides many benefits for a tree. In an urban environment, you can mimic this process by using an organic wood-chip mulch around trees. When applied correctly, your tree will benefit greatly.

Mulching benefits

- Reduces weed problems
- Reduces **soil compaction** and erosion
- Retains moisture
- Moderates soil temperatures
- Improves soil aeration and structure
- Looks good

Use composted mulch and apply it at a depth of 2 to 4 inches, depending on the soil. For soils that drain poorly, like clay, use 2 to 3 inches of mulch. Use 3 to 4 inches of mulch for better-draining soils. Spread the mulch wide, not deep. To avoid moist bark conditions and prevent decay, take care that the mulch doesn't touch the trunk of the tree.

At this point the plants have already stopped producing new growth, but roots are still able to absorb nutrients and store them for spring's growth push.

FERTILIZING SHRUBS

Fertilize shrub beds by broadcasting dry fertilizer over the soil surface and then watering thoroughly. Or scratch slow-release granular and coated fertilizers into the soil, following the manufacturer's instructions.

For broadleaf evergreen shrubs, such as rhododendrons and azaleas, use a fertilizer specific for acidic soil, since it usually contains minor elements in addition to nitrogen, phosphorus and potassium. Phosphorus helps with bud formation on azaleas and rhododendrons, while too much nitrogen can reduce flower buds.

MULCH

In the wild, the forest floor is covered with a natural mulch made up of decomposing leaves, twigs, branches and other plant and animal matter. Mulch keeps trees' roots cool in summer and warm in winter. It also keeps weeds down, helps the soil retain moisture, improves soil structure, and reduces erosion and compaction. Plus, it looks great. Studies have shown that wood-chip mulch can nearly double a tree's growth rate during the first few years after planting. Mulch also fertilizes as it breaks down.

After planting a tree, spread a 2- to 4-inch layer of mulch on the entire planting area, keeping it 3 inches away from the tree trunk. Mulch mounded against a tree's trunk can cause crown rot and make the tree vulnerable to disease and insect problems. The broader the mulched area the better — but don't make it too deep. Spread the mulch in the shape of a saucer, not a mound. This enables it to hold and distribute rainwater to the tree's roots. A moat of mulch will also protect an urban tree from damage caused by lawn mowers and weed eaters.

Wood chips are the most common type of tree mulch. Available from a variety of sources, they can often be obtained at no charge through your local municipality (especially after Christmas trees are recycled). The wood-chip mulch should be well-composted, not fresh, because breaking down fresh wood can use up nitrogen required by the plant. Compost made of decomposed plant matter (such as grass clippings, leaves, coffee grounds, fruits and veggies) also makes a fine mulch. Neither sawdust nor animal-based materials should be used as mulch, nor should you use a plastic liner under the mulch layer, as it will restrict water movement and limit oxygen availability in the root area.

Transplanting Mature Trees

If you want to landscape with mature trees and can't wait for young ones to grow, consider hiring a mechanical tree spade company. The tree contractor will know the best time of year to transplant your trees.

Generally, a tree over 10 feet tall or with a root ball greater than 3 feet in diameter usually requires mechanical planting. A **tree spade** is a mechanical device used to dig and transplant trees. The spade encircles the tree and large blades are forced into the ground diagonally around the tree to form a root ball. Because the size of the ball must be proportional to the size of the tree, there are various sizes of tree spades. Generally, the width of the root ball is a minimum of 10 inches in diameter per inch of trunk diameter.

When the planting hole is dug with a spade, the sides of the hole tend to glaze, which can inhibit root penetration. Be sure the sides are roughened up or loosened before the tree is planted. Trees greater than 4 inches in diameter are sometimes supported by **guying**, a technique used to secure large trees by wires that provides stronger support than staking.

A pole pruner allows you to prune branches that cannot be reached from the ground using other tools. The pole can range from 6 to 10 feet.

PRUNING

4

AWELL-GROOMED TREE PROVIDES aesthetic appeal, safety and investment value to the homeowner. All trees benefit from periodic pruning, which prolongs lifespan.

Trees that grow on boulevards and in our yards grow very differently than those that grow in the wild. In their natural habitat, trees face a lot of competition for light and space. As a result, they tend to grow straight up and have few side branches. In an urban environment, trees produce many **lateral branches** because they have the space to do so. Since urban trees have a greater number of branches, they develop more weak and problem branches that must be removed. Removing these branches has several benefits: it improves the tree's health, it decreases the number of potentially hazardous limbs and it enhances the aesthetic value of the tree.

Shade trees and ornamental trees can be costly to purchase due to their size and desirable features, so you do not want to destroy their natural appearance or compromise their health with incorrect pruning. The relatively low maintenance required by trees is one reason for their popularity, but ignoring an essential task can result in a great deal of extra work later on. Improper pruning of any kind does more harm than good and is an added source of stress to the tree.

Reasons for Pruning

Pruning involves the selective removal of branches for specific reasons. Ideally, the primary objective should be to promote, preserve or enhance plant health and structural integrity, while also maintaining natural form. It is also common to prune trees to accommodate human needs such

Pruning is used to:
- direct the growth of a limb or tree with a particular pruning cut;
- train a young tree to the desired form or structure;
- maintain mature tree form, size, health and appearance;
- ensure a safe environment;
- remove poor-quality wood, such as weak twigs, dead or diseased branches, and damaged stems;
- reduce production of shoots and **water sprouts**; and
- improve the quality of flowers, fruit, foliage and stems.

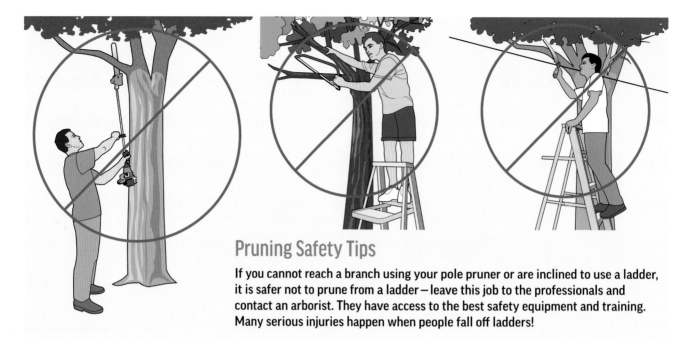

Pruning Safety Tips

If you cannot reach a branch using your pole pruner or are inclined to use a ladder, it is safer not to prune from a ladder — leave this job to the professionals and contact an arborist. They have access to the best safety equipment and training. Many serious injuries happen when people fall off ladders!

as height clearance, mitigating hazards, increasing light penetration or correcting a view.

A beautiful tree is a vigorous one, devoid of pests and diseases. Control of these health hazards is essential and it is best to remove the causes of these afflictions as early as possible. Pruning is one way to do this. Most diseases that attack trees enter through wounds and spread via the conducting tissue, killing off branches as the disease extends its hold. If a disease reaches the trunk, tree death usually occurs. The disease organism will travel beyond the wood it has killed and brown interior staining will appear in apparently healthy wood. When removing diseased wood, always cut back to sound wood — that is, to wood where there is no staining. Deadwood is unsightly and likely to break off, causing damage. Additionally, deadwood is a breeding ground for disease — always remove it.

All removal of large branches and pruning of tall trees should be completed by an arborist. Large branches are very heavy and amateurs cannot possibly control the branch's descent.

When to Prune

You do not need to prune your tree if it is not experiencing problems. This means that you may not have to prune every year. Late winter and early spring, when trees are still dormant, are good times to prune. During these periods you can see the arrangement of branches and you can expect large cuts to seal more quickly. The tree also has its greatest energy and nutrient reserves during these periods, which will help to minimize the risk of pest problems associated with wound entry.

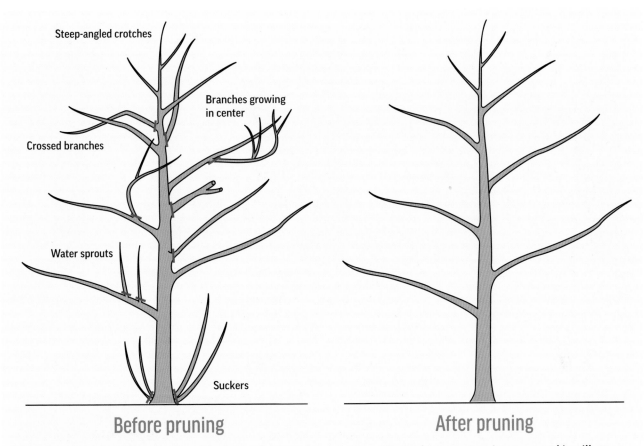

Before pruning

Steep-angled crotches

Branches growing in center

Crossed branches

Water sprouts

Suckers

After pruning

These are the things that you should look for when pruning your trees. Start when your tree is young, and it will grow with good structure and health.

Plant growth can be reduced if pruning takes place during or soon after initial growth flush, so pruning in this period is not recommended. You should not prune just before or after bud break. Also avoid heavy pruning in hot weather, as it can stress the plant. However, most routine pruning of weak, diseased or dead limbs can be accomplished at any time with little negative effect on the tree.

Before You Begin

Stand in front of your tree and assess its overall health and vigor. Look for signs of stress in the tree and take a moment to review what pruning corrections might be necessary, such as the removal of:

- dead, dying, broken, split or rubbing branches;
- **suckers** and water sprouts;
- long straggly branches;
- one or both branches that arise from a weak, tight V-shaped **branch union** with **included bark**;

> ✚ Basic pruning tools include pruning shears (or secateurs), lopping shears, a pruning saw (or handsaw), a pole pruner and a pole saw. These tools are available at most hardware and gardening centers. See page 74 for more details.

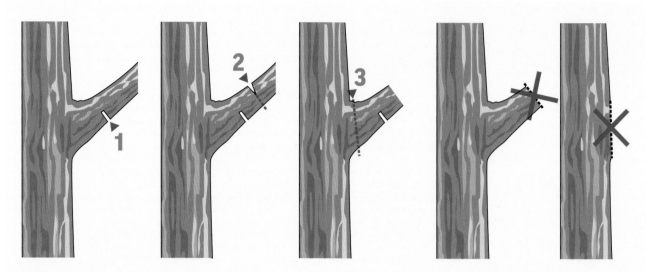

How to Prune a Large Branch

Three cuts are necessary to properly prune a large or heavy branch so that the bark does not peel or tear as it is removed.

1 The first cut should be made 1 to 2 feet from the trunk or parent limb. It should be an undercut about one-third of the way through the branch.

2 The second cut is made on top of the branch, farther out on the limb. This will allow the branch to break away without the bark tearing. Cut clear through to remove the branch.

3 The third cut removes the stub that is left. Make your final cut just outside the branch collar, leaving a nice clean cut that protrudes just beyond the ridge.

- multiple leaders where a central leader is both desirable and characteristic of the species;
- a portion of the vigorous laterals on a conifer to maintain dominance of the central leader;
- selected living branches throughout the crown to accomplish uniform light **thinning**;
- spent flower heads; and
- branches that have been weakened or irreparably damaged by insect or disease attack.

Heavy sucker growth or water sprouts signal that the tree is stressed. The tree produces these fast-growing shoots in order to capture energy and produce nutrients that it is not receiving in sufficient supply. Look for excessive deadwood in the crown that could be caused by a root problem. Also look at the size of the leaves and the amount of growth the twigs have sprouted in a year. This will give you an idea of the strength of the tree. Leaves that are smaller than normal and stunted twig growth are signs of stress or poor health. Finally, check for insect damage and disease. Has there been excessive defoliation or **dieback** in the crown?

All of these factors are important because they will determine how you will prune the tree. By removing branches, you are removing some of the

During winter, inspect your trees for pruning work that you'll need to do in the spring, such as cutting back excessive suckers growing from the base of the tree.

tree's ability to produce energy through photosynthesis, a process that involves the leaves converting energy into nutrients for the plant. Also, there is food stored in the branches that will be lost when they are pruned.

Keep this in mind when pruning because, although trees can be very resilient, you may send a stressed tree into a downward spiral with a severe pruning, which may kill the tree.

Consider the following issues in order to ensure that your tree is pruned properly and remains healthy and aesthetically pleasing:

- Know what kind of tree you are going to prune.
- Know the tree's growth habits and its natural shape and appearance in order to maintain shape.
- Know how to make a proper cut.
- Determine your objectives for pruning.
- Determine what tools you will need.
- Consider what time of year it is.
- Consider whether it is a young tree or a mature tree.

Hand primers or secateurs are used on small trees for cuts up to a ½ inch in diameter.

Pruning Tools

IN ORDER TO PRUNE your trees and shrubs properly and efficiently, use the following recommended tools.

Pruning shears

Hand pruners, or secateurs, are used on small trees and shrubs to make cuts up to a ½ inch in diameter. The bypass-style pruning shears are the best. These shears have a curved blade that cuts by passing against a curved bill. Anvil-style shears have a straight blade that can crush branch tissue and leave stubs when cut against a flat anvil, and are not recommended. To make a proper cut, always place the blade close to the parent stem and cut upward. When pruning back to a bud, make the cut a ¼ inch above the active bud at the same angle as the bud. If you cut any closer, the bud will dry out. If you cut any higher, a stub is left, subjecting the branch to dieback.

Lopping shears

These shears are used in the same way as hand shears, but they have longer handles and can cut branches up to 1¼ inches in diameter. Lopping shears work well for cutting out old canes (woody stems) to rejuvenate the plant.

To help revitalize your plant, use lopping shears to thin out older, thicker woody branches that have a diameter up to 1¼ inch.

Pruning saw

A pruning saw (handsaw) is necessary for pruning small trees. Use it to cut branches greater than 1 to 1½ inches in diameter. A handsaw has a 13- or 14-inch tri-cut blade that is very sharp and provides a fast, clean cut with little effort. When the saw is dull, simply replace the blade. Wear leather gloves when using a pruning saw and be careful to avoid cutting yourself with its razor-sharp blade.

A pruning saw is a tool necessary for pruning small trees. It can cut branches greater than 1½ inches in diameter.

Pole pruner

A pole pruner is a great tool that allows you to prune branches that cannot be reached from the ground. A pole pruner can make small cuts near branch ends that would be awkward with a hand-saw. The pole pruner should have a bypass-style pruner head, similar to that of hand shears. The pole length can range from 6 to 10 feet and extensions are available to reach other heights. You should not use a pole pruner to cut any more than the head will allow, usually 1 to 1½ inches. Also try to avoid cutting deadwood with it, as it is hard on the blade.

Pole saw

Another useful pole tool is the pole saw. It uses the same tri-cut blade as the handsaw for a fast, clear cut. Use it to prune branches larger than 1½ inches in diameter to remove deadwood, and to prune stubs and broken branches.

When using pole tools, avoid cutting large branches directly over your head. Keep your cuts small and manageable, and let an arborist handle the bigger pruning jobs.

You should also consider hiring an arborist if the type of pruning you're doing requires the use of a chainsaw. Chainsaws are dangerous tools best left to skilled professionals.

Keep your tools clean and sharp so that they will leave clean, accurate cuts. Dull tools will leave

A pole pruner allows you to prune branches that cannot be reached from the ground using other tools. The pole can range from 6 to 10 feet.

a ragged appearance and could damage the tree's bark. When pruning diseased branches you will have to sterilize your tools between cuts to avoid spreading the disease throughout the tree or to other trees. Use disinfectants such as Lysol, alcohol or bleach. Dilute them in a 1-to-10 ratio with water and spray the tools or dip them in the solution. In both cases, be sure to completely cover the entire tool to properly disinfect it. These solutions can cause tools to rust, so carefully rinse or dry your tools after use and oil them when stored. Choose good-quality tools and maintain them, and your pruning jobs will be much easier.

A pole saw is another useful tool for reaching into the canopy. You should wear gloves, protective eyewear and a helmet when you are pruning large branches over your head.

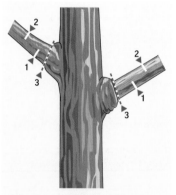

The three-cut method prevents the bark from tearing. A proper cut just outside the branch collar is necessary for the third cut.

Proper Pruning Technique

Use your secateurs (or pruning shears) to remove branches and other plant parts up to a ½ inch in diameter. Prune small branches ¼ inch above an outward-facing bud to direct new growth away from the canopy interior.

When pruning a larger branch with a handsaw, three cuts are necessary to avoid having the weight of the branch tear the bark at the point where the branch meets the main stem: an undercut, followed by an overcut, then the final cut. International Society of Arboriculture practice recommends the following steps:

1. The first cut undercuts the limb 1 or 2 feet out from the parent branch or trunk. Cut only one-third of the way through the branch. The undercut prevents the bark from stripping.
2. The next step is to make a top cut slightly farther out on the limb. Cut clear through to remove the branch. The limb will drop smoothly when the weight is released.
3. The final cut removes the stub. It should be clean and straight. It is important that this cut is made properly so the tree can seal over the wound. Look for the natural swelling where the branch meets the main stem. This is called the branch bark ridge. Slightly out from that is the **branch collar** where the cut should be made, leaving a small neat shoulder that protrudes just beyond the ridge. Do not leave a large stub or cut too close. A flush cut will create a bigger wound than necessary and won't seal over.

Start any pruning job by removing deadwood. Deadwood is easy to spot during the growing season because it bears no leaves and snaps easily,

CODIT stands for compartmentalization of decay in trees. When a wound is created in a tree – by pruning, for example – the tree has the ability to prevent decay from spreading. The tree forms four barriers that prevent decay from spreading inward, outward, vertically and horizontally. This ability is unique to trees and, as such, pruning paint isn't recommended or required.

revealing no green under the bark. After removing deadwood, prune your trees to improve their structure, making them stronger and more attractive.

A thinning cut removes a branch at the junction of the stem or parent limb, or shortens a primary branch to a lateral shoot large enough to assume **apical dominance** (to support life). The remaining lateral should have the diameter of at least one-third the diameter of the portion being removed (the remaining part of the branch should be at least one-third the size of the portion removed).

Coniferous Evergreens

Coniferous evergreens don't readily produce new shoots from old wood. Pruning beyond the foliage into older wood will result in dieback and decline. Limit pruning to the portion of the crown that has foliage. The best time to prune evergreens is while they are actively growing or while new growth is still soft.

Pines and spruces need little pruning. Remove deadwood and co-dominant leaders. If you want a dense, compact appearance, you must "candle" the tree. Before the needles come out, head back the new shoots on pines with hand shears or by pinching off the shoots. If you want compact growth on your spruce, head back the terminal and side branches to the buds in late winter or early spring, before new growth emerges.

Training your trees by corrective pruning is the best way to maintain and ensure their proper structure and health. It is better to make smaller cuts when the trees are young than to try to correctively prune a mature tree.

Pruning Young Trees

Pruning at the time of planting is not recommended, except to remove broken branches and deadwood. If necessary, a central trunk or leader should be developed by removing competing leaders. Do not cut back to compensate for root loss. Do not remove lower branches or perform any crown thinning until the tree is established.

If young trees are trained or pruned to promote good structure, they will likely remain vibrant for longer than trees that have not been similarly pruned. Defects can be removed, a single dominant leader can be selected and branches can be spaced out well along the main trunk. Well-pruned young trees have a lower potential for structural failure at maturity and require less maintenance later on.

To correct poor structure at the time of planting, start structural pruning by shortening upright stems that compete with the leader. This directs future growth into one dominant leader because pruned stems are slower growing.

The process of training young trees, as recommended by the International Society of Arboriculture in its *Arborists' Certification Study Guide*, includes five simple steps:

1. Remove broken, dead, dying or damaged branches.
2. Select and establish a dominant leader. There should be only one leader, usually the strongest vertical stem. Competing stems should be cut back or removed.

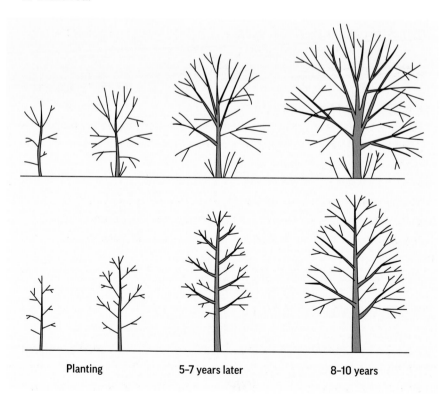

Planting   5–7 years later   8–10 years

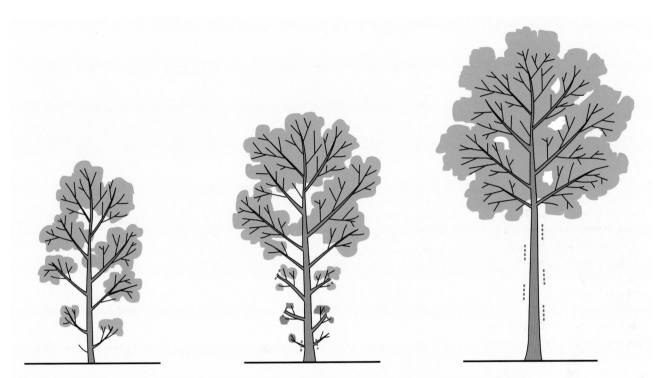

The lower branches on the trunk of a young tree help develop a strong trunk and proper trunk taper. Leave them on for the first four or five years before pruning them to the lowest permanent branch.

3. Select and establish the lowest permanent branch. The height of this branch should be determined by the location and intended function of the tree.
4. Select and establish **scaffold branches**, the permanent and structural branches of your tree. Choose based on good attachment, appropriate size and spacing in relation to other branches.
5. Select temporary branches below the lowest permanent branch. These branches should be retained temporarily because they help provide energy back to the trunk and provide shade to young trunk tissues. Smaller temporary branches can be left intact because they help form good trunk taper, which provides stability for the tree. Larger branches should be pruned.

This training process should be spread out over many years, if practical. A widely accepted goal is to remove no more than 25 percent of the canopy in any one year. Proper training can be accomplished by removing much less.

Pruning Mature Trees

Factors to consider when pruning mature trees include site, time of year, species, size, growth habit, vitality and maturity. As a general rule, mature trees are less tolerant of severe pruning than young ones. Large, mature

Before

After lion tailing

Thinning a branch properly involves maintaining well-spaced limbs so there is an even distribution of foliage along the whole branch. If you remove too many inner and lower branches and foliage on a limb, too much weight is concentrated on the ends and branch taper is discouraged. This makes for a weak branch that is prone to failure during storms. This poor practice is referred to as "lion tailing" and should be avoided.

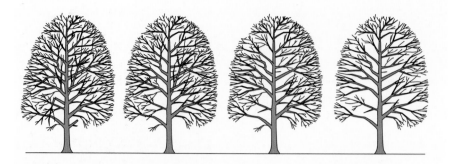

Periodic pruning for specific purposes such as deadwood, branch spacing, interfering limbs or poor branch unions, makes for healthy and beautiful trees. The benefits of such activity are seen after a tree has been properly pruned.

trees should require little routine pruning. The older and larger a tree becomes, the less energy it has in reserve to close wounds and defend against decay or insect attack. The pruning of mature trees is usually limited to the removal of dead branches to reduce the severity of structural defects.

Pruning Tips: What *Not* to Do

Topping trees is the worst form of pruning possible. It involves cutting back tree branches to stubs or lateral branches that are not large enough to assume dominance. Topping is harmful and will negatively impact the health, structure and maintenance of your trees. Homeowners sometimes want to top their trees because they feel they have become too large and may damage a home or other structures. Nevertheless, topping trees creates a greater potential for hazard in the long run.

Topping disfigures trees. The tree's natural branching structure is destroyed and will never fully regain its natural form. When a topped tree is without leaves during the dormant winter months it looks unsightly. With leaves it is simply a dense ball of foliage, lacking a nice flowing shape.

Topping depletes the tree of stored energy reserves and reduces the tree's ability to produce energy, as a large percentage of its leaves are removed. The stressed tree will form a growth of multiple shoots below each topping cut. These shoots grow quickly, are very weak and are prone to breaking in the wind. Also, stubs left from topping usually decay, causing wood to rot.

Severely topped trees are more susceptible to insect and disease infestations. Additionally, the sun can damage the bark, causing **cankers**, bark splitting and the death of some branches.

Topping will cost you money in the long run. It is a high-maintenance practice that needs to be revisited every couple of years. If the tree dies, it will have to be removed. If weak growth is damaged in a storm, it will

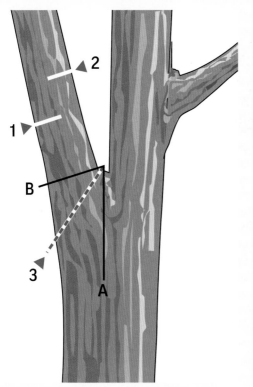
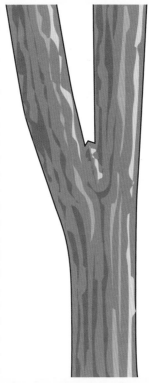
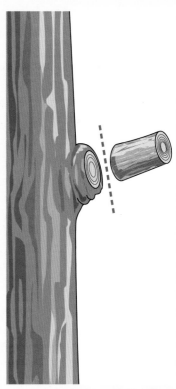

When removing a co-dominant stem or V-shaped crotch, first remove most of the stem by undercutting it and then follow with a top cut. The angle of your first cut should bisect the angle formed by the branch bark ridge (B), and an imaginary line made perpendicular to the growth of the leader being removed.

Co-dominant stems have a weak point of attachment and are prone to failure. Remove or cut back the stems, preferably when the tree is young.

To prune a dead stub, cut the stub back to the collar of living tissue, removing only the dead portion.

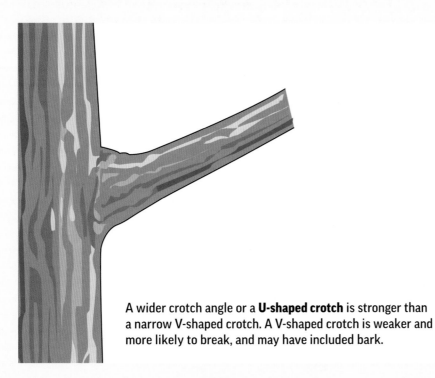
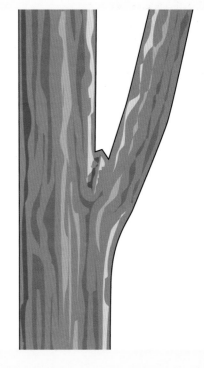

A wider crotch angle or a **U-shaped crotch** is stronger than a narrow V-shaped crotch. A V-shaped crotch is weaker and more likely to break, and may have included bark.

A shrub may need renovation when all of its new foliage is simply tall, bare stems.

A **flush cut** removes a branch right to the trunk, leaving no stub at all. Never cut any branch flush. Flush cuts remove the natural protection zones a tree needs to prevent invasion by insect pests and disease.

Stub cuts, the opposite of flush cuts, can be just as harmful. A stub is what remains of a branch after the cut. Long or short, dead stubs are a fuel source for disease and a safe harbor for insects.

Do not apply pruning paint to a wound after a pruning cut. When a proper pruning cut is made, the tree has a natural ability to compartmentalize the wound and prevent decay from entering it in any direction. The tree's cambium layer will then produce **callus** tissue around and over the wound. When pruning a stub that has formed callus tissue, only the dead portion of the stub should be removed, preserving the healthy callus.

Pruning Shrubs

Shrub pruning is very similar to shade-tree pruning. Start by removing dead, dying and diseased branches. Then make thinning cuts to remove some of the older stems or canes. This will encourage younger sprouts from the root crown, which will be more vigorous and produce more flowers. Heading cuts that pertain only to shrub pruning may be necessary to shape the plant, and will control and direct growth. Heading cuts must be made at a lateral branch or a bud. Head back to a lateral or a bud that points in the direction you want the plant to grow. If you want a more spreading plant, cut back to an outward-facing bud or lateral. For an upright plant, cut back to an inward-facing bud.

Prune spring-flowering shrubs once the flowers have died. Prune summer- or fall-flowering shrubs during dormancy.

Certain shrubs that have grown too large can be trained into small trees,

After pruning, you will need to remove brush that has been cut. Some wood, such as cedar, is excellent for making garden structures such as arbors or furniture.

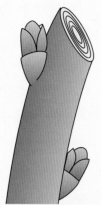

Correct

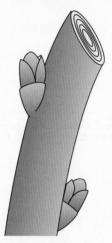

Excessive stub

Too close

A proper cut for shrubs should be at a 45-degree angle about a ¼ inch above an active bud. If the cut is too close, it will interfere with bud growth and dry out. If the cut is too far out, the branch will die back.

Some shrubs can be grown as small multi-stemmed trees by selecting major stems to become trunks and pruning the lower branches to the desired height.

such as the amur maple, the Russian olive and the smoke bush. Remove their lower branches and tidy their interiors.

Shearing Versus Pruning

Shearing removes a portion of the current season's growth and should be done one or more times per year. It gives a structured, formal, hard appearance, as foliage is concentrated on the perimeter of the plant. The dense outer canopy reduces light and air penetration. If a portion of the plant became damaged, ugly holes could appear due to a lack of foliar growth (presence of leaves) within the plant.

Pruning removes plant parts prior to the current growth season. This tends to rejuvenate the plant. It also provides a more natural shape and improves overall health.

Shrub renovation

A shrub may need renovation when:

- it has been neglected and has grown too large;
- it is flowering too high;
- it is too sprawling and takes up too much room; and
- all new foliage is tall bare stems.

To renovate a shrub, head back the entire plant to between 6 and 12 inches above the ground. Renovating in early spring before buds break will result in rapid plant regrowth.

Shearing your shrubs gives them a structured formal appearance.

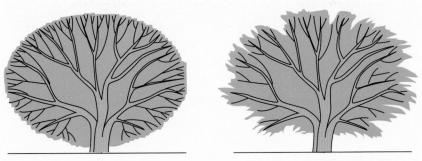

These are the growth habits of sheared and pruned shrubs. Shearing provides a more formal appearance, while pruned shrubs have a more natural, informal appearance.

Hedges

Prune hedges so the plants are wide at the bottom and narrow at the top. This will allow light to reach the lower foliage and result in healthier plants. This method also minimizes the potential for snow and ice loading.

Begin pruning when hedge plants are young to ensure a desirable shape. You can maintain hedges by either shearing or pruning.

A hedge should be wider at its bottom than at its top. This way, light will be able to reach the whole plant to help keep it full and dense.

Inspect your trees regularly for signs of stress caused by weather conditions such as drought, invasive species or disease.

DIAGNOSING TREE
PROBLEMS

ONCE YOU HAVE TAKEN the time to choose your tree, plant it carefully in an appropriate space and carry out tasks such as mulching and watering, you are ready to enjoy its spectacular natural beauty for years to come. You have made an investment that will benefit your community and increase the monetary and aesthetic value of your home.

However, your tree's strength and vigor can be compromised by factors such as stress, disease or insects. Although most trees will thrive in a yard if properly cared for, you should be on the lookout for any irregularities in your tree's health. To be healthy, a tree requires sufficient water and light, and a proper balance of nutrients. Trees cope with environmental stresses such as shading and competition for water and nutrients within their native environment by adjusting their growth and development patterns according to the resources available. When you see changes in your tree's appearance, examine it carefully. After identifying specific symptoms of damage and finding the cause, you can decide how to treat the problem.

Biotic and Abiotic Plant Problems

Plant health problems fall into two basic categories: **biotic** and **abiotic**. Living agents such as insects, mites and animals, and diseases such as fungi, bacteria and viruses, are the cause of biotic problems. These health problems are considered infectious because they can spread from one tree to the next.

Non-living agents (or abiotic agents) are non-infectious. Abiotic disorders are caused by weather conditions, soil conditions, and man-made physical and chemical disturbances to the air and environment. Stress

> ✚ There are two categories of plant health problems: biotic and abiotic problems. Living agents, such as insects, mites and animals, and diseases such as fungi, bacteria and viruses, cause biotic problems. Biotic problems are infectious. Abiotic problems are caused by weather and soil conditions, and by man-made physical and chemical disturbances to the air and environment. Abiotic problems are non-infectious, but they comprise the majority of tree health problems.

Stress from drought can cause leaves to change their color, appear lackluster and drop early.

resulting from abiotic disorders can weaken plants and leave them susceptible to biotic disorders. Abiotic disorders comprise the majority of tree health problems. In fact, 70 to 90 percent of all plant problems are the result of environmental conditions such as soil compaction, high or low temperatures, drought, air pollution, nutrient deficiencies, herbicides, root collar disorders, mechanical injury, flooding and poor species selection. Often, plant health problems can be a combination of infectious and non-infectious problems.

Excessive water sprouts are an indicator of stress.

How to Make a Diagnosis

Proper diagnosis starts with careful examination.

- Start by correctly identifying the plant. This should help establish whether your tree's growth rate is normal or not. Also, many biotic and abiotic conditions are specific to certain tree types.
- The next step is to examine the site. Consider the area the tree is growing in. Are soil and drainage adequate? Has there been any activity that has changed the site by changing the grade or compacting the soil? What were the recent climate conditions? Drought, excessive rain and extreme temperature fluctuations can all influence tree health. Were

The Disease Triangle

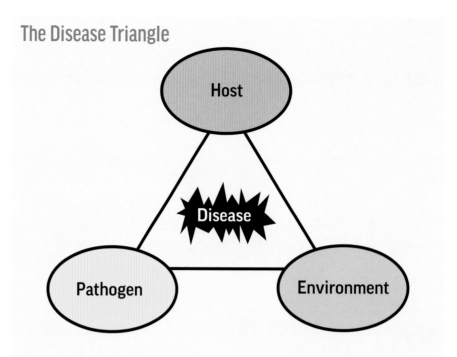

A disease can develop when all parts of the disease triangle are present. This includes a susceptible host plant, a pathogen and favorable environmental conditions. Moisture and temperature contribute to the development and severity of the disease.

any pesticides used recently or in previous years? What was growing on the site previously? Were those plants also experiencing problems? Could the same problems be affecting the current plants?

- Note symptoms by looking at leaves, shoots, roots and the root collar. You will often notice changes to foliage first. Examine the growth and color of your tree's leaves. Yellow-green foliage can be indicative of nutrient deficiencies. Dead leaves at the top of the tree are usually the result of mechanical or environmental root stress. Twisted and curled leaves could be the result of herbicides or insects. Look for insects and evidence of insects, such as chewing, mining, **skeletonizing** and insect waste (such as **honeydew**). Root tips should be white and fleshy. Brown and black tips indicate overly wet soil or the presence of root-rotting organisms.

- Examine the trunk and branches. Look for wounds, blisters, cankers, feeding insects or any other abnormalities. Low wounds can result from mechanical damage by lawn mowers or string trimmers. Small holes can indicate the presence of **boring** insects. Weather can cause sunscald or frost cracks, and rodents can chew and damage bark. Excessive water sprouts and sucker growth can indicate stress on the tree from severe pruning or poor growing conditions. Examine how the trunk enters the soil. If the trunk flare isn't evident, the tree may be planted too deep. If the trunk is flat or indented on one side, it probably has a girdling root.

Damaging insects fall into three categories: boring insects like the European bark beetle, chewing insects such as the gypsy moth and the Eastern tent caterpillar, and sucking insects such as aphids and mites.

Correct diagnosis of plant problems requires a careful examination of the situation. The International Society of Arboriculture recommends the following tips:

• Accurately identify the plant, because many insects and disease are plant-specific.
• Look for a pattern of abnormality.
• Carefully examine the landscape for other existing problems.
• Examine the roots of your tree for any discoloration.
• Check the trunk and branches for wounds that provide entrance for pathogens.
• Note the portion and appearance of affected leaves.

The treatment method used for a particular insect or disease problem will depend on the species involved, the extent of the problem and a variety of other factors specific to the situation and local regulations. Always consult a professional if you have any doubt about the nature of the problem or proper treatment.

How Your Climate Impacts Trees

Your climate could pose an abiotic problem.

General climate regions

Coastal Pacific Northwest: Mild winters and summers, along with moist conditions (except for late summer) allow homeowners to choose from a long list of native and exotic trees. Many conifers also grow rapidly in high humidity.

Mediterranean California: Similar to those of the Mediterranean, the mild winters and warm dry summers of California allow numerous native and exotic trees to thrive.

Southwest: In an area with extreme heat and aridity, the emphasis is on drought-tolerant species and desert natives tolerant of these dry conditions.

Midwest and plains: This inland region has winters comparable to those in the Northeast, but with colder temperatures. It also has less moisture, higher winds and hotter summers.

Northeast and Appalachians: Well-known for the colorful fall foliage of its native trees, this region has cold winters and mild, humid summers.

Southeast: The geography within this region includes swampy lowlands and drier, upland hardwood forests; the region is moist with mild winters and long, hot summers.

Ozone pollution

Air pollution is carried across the land by wind, air currents and moving vehicles. Ozone, an air pollutant, can be harmful to trees. Excessive ozone in the lower atmosphere is caused by car emissions, the energy it takes to warm and cool houses and buildings, and power plants. Gases are released when coal and gasoline are burned; when mixed with oxygen they create ozone.

Some trees are more tolerant to pollution exposure than others. Ozone, which enters trees through small openings in their leaves, reduces the amount of food the tree can make through photosynthesis. It can kill or weaken a tree and make it vulnerable to pests and other debilitating conditions. Leaves can burn at the edges and spots will appear on their surfaces.

If air pollution is a problem in the area where you live, consider choosing pollution-tolerant trees and avoid those that are less tolerant. (See p. 41.)

Flood

Flooding can have disastrous effects on the landscape. It may wear away topsoil or dump silt and debris over the root zones of your trees. Flooded soil deprives tree roots of the oxygen required for nourishment. Most tree roots are found in the top foot of soil because that's where most of the oxygen is located. When water fills up the air pockets in the soil, there is no room left for oxygen. Wet roots are also susceptible to rot. As they give out, leaves sag or drop and limbs die back. After a flood, wait a year before pruning any branches to see if the limbs show signs of recovery. Fertilizer may help restore vitality.

If flooding is common in your area, consider incorporating compost or other organic matter into the soil, which will help to improve drainage. You may also want to consider employing a landscaper or architect to install a piping drainage system to carry off excess water.

Drought

A lack of water in soil decreases a tree's vigor and may be fatal to its health. Drought destroys feeder roots and root hairs, which absorb water. Located in the top foot of soil, these roots are quickly affected by moisture loss. Such stress to the tree may result in wilting leaves, scorch or leaf loss. Spider mites, leaf-eating insects or wood borers are active in hot, dry weather and invade stressed trees.

If your area is susceptible to drought, plant trees that are more tolerant of this condition, such as hawthorns, green ashes, Kentucky coffee trees, junipers, American plums, and limber and mugo pines. During periods of drought, water newly planted trees weekly. Recently transplanted trees need plenty of water to become established. Newly

Tree trunks broken down by high winds and lightning during a summer thunder storm..

A freezing rain storm damaged thousands of trees and caused power outages in the Greater Toronto Area in 2013.

planted balled-and-burlapped trees are particularly vulnerable, since many of their feeder roots were cut when harvested.

If drought is infrequent, keep your trees well-watered during dry spells. It's better to water deeply — for 30 minutes at various points around the tree's drip line — and less frequently instead of a light sprinkling every few days.

Leaf scorch

If you see the edges of leaves turn yellow and then brown it is evidence of leaf scorch. Leaf scorch is often the result of hot weather, dry winds and dry soils. It can lead to pest and disease problems as it weakens the tree's vitality — and vice versa. Trees that develop leaf scorch include lindens, oaks, ashes and maples. During dry periods, water your trees deeply and mulch them to conserve moisture and to help prevent leaf scorch.

Pine and spruce conifers and broad-leaf evergreens such as rhododendron and mountain laurel are vulnerable to leaf scorch in winter as well as in summer, particularly on sunny or windy winter days, when the damage is known as winter burn. Keep these plants well-watered throughout the growing season and into the fall to prevent winter burn and be aware of the path of prevailing winter winds. Consider wrapping evergreens in burlap or building a wooden structure to protect them from harsh winds.

Wind

The branches that are most susceptible to breaking in the wind are the heavy ones that join with the trunk at an acute angle. You can prevent breakage by choosing well-formed trees or by hiring an arborist to help shape your tree to withstand wind damage.

Evergreens continue losing water through their leaves during the winter, so wind protection is important. Make sure to water your evergreen trees and shrubs well into the fall until the ground freezes, which helps prevent the foliage from turning brown. Selecting proper planting locations will also help avoid damage. In southern Canada and the United States, prevailing winds move from the west or southwest towards the east or northeast. Consider building a wind fence out of stakes and burlap to block the prevailing winter wind and the southern and southwestern exposure of evergreens.

Snow and ice

Snow and ice on trees create a winter wonderland effect, but too much weight can be detrimental to the trees' health. The weight of snow can crush evergreens and break apart limbs on deciduous trees. Ice-coated trunks and branches can also snap. You can help avoid winter damage by brushing off snow and pruning any apparent damage. Trees that are well-pruned can better combat snow and ice than those with weak branch crotches or multiple leaders.

Sunscald

Thin-barked trees, such as maples, ashes, honey locusts, lindens and willows, are susceptible to sunscald, which occurs during winter when the sun sits lower in the sky. The sun warms the south and southwest sides of tree trunks and kills the inner bark of young deciduous trees, especially when winter days are warm and sunny and nights are below freezing. Sunscald happens frequently in parts of the Southwestern United States.

Lightning

Although you can't prevent a lightning strike, you can plant trees that are less vulnerable to strikes, such as birches and beeches. Among the more at-risk trees are pines, oaks and maples. Their height and opposite branching patterns make them more susceptible to lightning injury.

External damage from lightning strikes includes strips of bark hanging from the tree and broken branches; internal injuries include burned roots and systematic damage inside the tree. If lightning strikes a tree and there does not appear to be much harm, you can help rejuvenate the tree by cutting off hanging bark, fertilizing its soil, keeping its root zone mulched and watering it during dry weather.

A drought-resistant Utah juniper tree sits on top of a sandstone ridge in Colorado National Monument.

Most Common Tree-Damaging Insects

Sometimes insects that cause damage to trees can be seen doing the damage; however, in many cases the damage is more visible than the pest. This is because some pests, like spider mites, are too small to see or, by the time damage is detected, the insects may be gone.

1. Larva and adult wood borers
2. Leaf-chewing insect damage
3. Bark beetle
4. Mites
5. Lace bug
6. Scale insects
7. Tent caterpillar egg mass
8. Aphids
9. Serpentine leaf miners
10. Root-feeding white grub

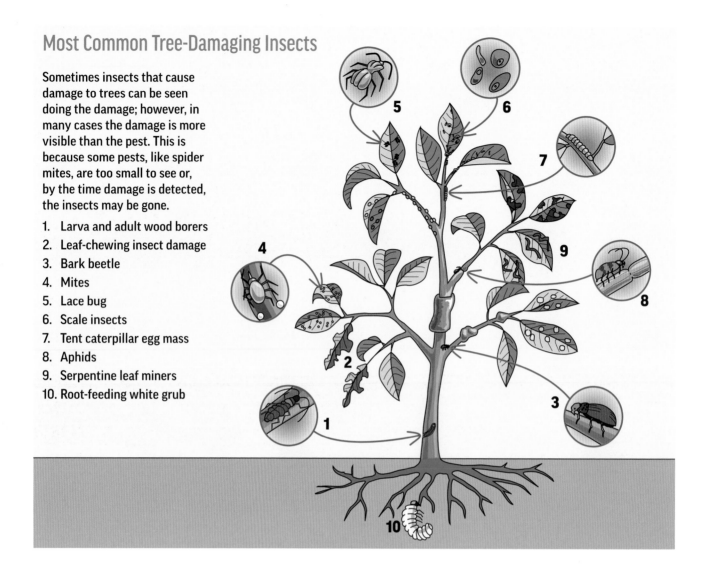

Insects

Most insects found in your yard do not damage ornamental trees and shrubs. Many insects are considered beneficial because they help with pollination or prey on other damaging insects. Often an insect problem will be secondary to problems brought on by stress or disease. Killing all insects, without regard to their kind and function, can be detrimental to tree health.

However, most tree species have at least one pest that causes damage. Many of the serious pests attacking ornamental plants in North America were imported by accident on plant material. The gypsy moth, the elm leaf beetle, the Japanese beetle and the European elm bark beetle are all imported pests.

Insects can cause damage by boring into the tree, chewing the leaves and sucking the sap from leaves.

Invasive insects can affect your trees in various ways.

BORING INSECTS

Boring insects are insect larvae that chew and tunnel under a tree's bark and into the wood. These near-invisible pests affect twigs, limbs and trunks. Look for small holes in the branches or trunks where the insects enter, which may be accompanied by bits of sawdust nearby. Boring insects eat inner bark, phloem and xylem, disrupting the flow of water and nutrients from the roots to the canopy, which causes considerable damage to healthy trees. Young trees and softwood types are particularly vulnerable to these pests.

Borers are likely to attack trees that are already weakened and are often considered a secondary problem. Symptoms of borer damage are a thin crown, crown dieback and a noticeable decline in plant vigor. Examples of boring inserts are the bronze birch borer and the European bark beetle.

CHEWING INSECTS

Chewing insects, or defoliators, eat plant tissue such as leaves, flowers, buds and twigs. Some will eat the entire leaf, while others will skeletonize the leaf by eating the tissue between its veins or hollow out the leaf, feeding between the leaf's surfaces. These latter pests are called leaf miners. A healthy deciduous tree can withstand complete defoliation in one season; however, complete defoliation two years in a row could seriously harm it. Conifers often die after one season of defoliation. Keep trees that have had heavy defoliation well-watered and mulched, and make sure the required nutrients are available in the soil.

Common defoliators include caterpillars, such as the gypsy moth and the Eastern tent caterpillar, sawflies, leaf beetles, Japanese beetles, birch leaf miners and cedar leaf miners.

SUCKING INSECTS

Sucking insects have piercing mouthparts that penetrate leaves, twigs, branches, flowers or fruit and then feed on the plant's juices by sucking out the sap. Signs of such damage include fading leaf color, curling and twisting leaves, wilting foliage and malformed flowers. Some common sucking insects are aphids, leafhoppers, mites, mealybugs and scales. Aphids may secrete a sugary substance called honeydew, which attracts ants and flies and is a nuisance when it covers objects located beneath branches. Honeydew also promotes the growth of sooty mold, a black and unsightly fungus. Heavy infestations of aphids stunt tree growth.

Mites, often referred to as spider mites, are arachnids. They can cause foliage bronzing and leaf drop. Mites reproduce rapidly in hot, dry weather. They are very small and hard to see, but you can diagnose mites by shaking a branch over a white sheet of paper.. Mites will land on the paper and can be seen crawling about. A heavy infestation of spider mites, active during the summer months, will leave silvery webbing in the affected area.

Common Insects

Aphids

Small, pear-shaped, soft-bodied insects, aphids live in colonies and suck sap from leaves and stems. There are many different aphid species and each is adapted to feed on one or a group of tree species. Most trees are tolerant and, while aphids usually do not cause significant damage, they can weaken trees and make them susceptible to other pests. Aphids produce a sticky liquid called honeydew that drips onto leaves, stems and objects beneath the tree. Honeydew attracts ants, wasps and flies. Aphids may cause leaf curling, bud distortion, gall formations and twig dieback.

Ladybugs and lacewings are natural enemies of aphids and help control the aphid population. Heavy rainfall can also reduce aphid populations and watering them with a hose will produce a similar effect. Hose the tree in the morning so that its leaves remain dry during the day; damp leaves promote other foliar disease development. If aphid damage is persistent, use an insecticidal soap spray or check with your local garden center for a sticky band that inhibits the movement of ants that promote aphid colonies when it is banded around the tree trunk.

Aphids on pine needles.

Above and below: A birch ash leaf miner fly.

Birch leaf miner

Included in a group of insects known as sawflies, the birch leaf miner is a very small pest that is black and can be seen hovering or crawling over birch tree leaves in the spring. The fly lays eggs in young leaves, which hatch into larvae a few days later and feed, causing damage to the leaves of birch trees. The larvae tunnel underneath the surface of the leaf by devouring leaf cells. After about 15 days of growth, the larvae fall to the ground and pupate into flies, starting the process again. Birch leaf miners prefer young shoots on newly planted or overly pruned trees, or shoots from the stems of distressed trees.

Leaf miner activity may occur between May and September. The pests' preferred hosts are paper birch and gray birch trees, and the leaf damage they cause appears as reddish-brown blotches. "Mined" leaves often stay on the tree until autumn, giving the tree a "brownish" overall appearance. Leaf miner damage is primarily aesthetic; however, a tree may decline with the addition of other pests and stressors.

Pruning birch trees may create new shoots that attract leaf miners, so it's best to avoid over-pruning. Choose resistant birch tree species, such as river birch, black birch and yellow birch. Leaf miners' natural enemies include parasitic wasps. You can support the population of natural enemies by not using broadcast pesticides.

Elm bark beetle

The native elm bark beetle has the ability to transmit Dutch elm disease (DED). Adult beetles emerge from under the bark of elm trees in early spring and feed on the bark of twigs, often at the crotches of the trees. They carry the DED fungus from infected trees to healthy ones. They chew

101

Diseased elm tree to be destroyed – can only find images of elm bark beetle tracks in old wood, not live trees.

through the inner bark, forming a 2- to 3-inch (5- to 7-centimeter) long gallery where they lay their eggs. The larvae hatch and feed on the inner bark, carving tunnels perpendicular to the egg gallery. The fungus spreads through these tunnels to the tree's water-conducting system. Mature larvae pupate in the bark and the insects emerge as adult beetles in the spring. In Canada there is typically one generation of elm bark beetles per year, but in southern areas there are often two.

Elm bark beetles only feed and breed on elm trees. They do not cause serious physical damage to the trees, but they are significant as pests because of their ability to transmit DED. The most effective control is to destroy or reduce the beetles' breeding habitat by removing dead or dying elm trees and destroying the wood. (Note: Do not store or transport elm firewood if it has not previously been de-barked.)

Carpenter ants

Unlike termites, **carpenter ants** do not eat wood. Rather, they nest in wet wood in the cavities of trees. The presence of these pests is usually a sign of wood decay. Carpenter ants are large black insects that live in colonies. They are particularly active at night when they feed on honeydew from aphids, in addition to other insects, fruit and garbage.

The carpenter ants chew moist wood to create more room for their expanding colonies. One sign of their existence is the presence of chewed wood around the nest entrance, a sawdust-like frass. Frequently found nesting in damp wood in buildings, carpenter ants make rustling noises loud enough to hear through walls.

Decaying trees, remnant stumps, uncovered firewood, logs and wood structures such as fences or decks are all outdoor sites that may support carpenter ants. If you have carpenter ants in a tree, look for frass around the tree base to locate possible nesting places. You'll usually locate the nest directly above the ejected frass. The nest in the tree indicates the presence of wood decay, which could potentially result in structural failure. This may require pruning or removal.

Invasive Insect Pests

A species is **invasive** when it is both non-native to the ecosystem where it is found and capable of causing harm to the environment, economy and people. Invasive species often compete so successfully in new ecosystems that they displace **native species** and disrupt important ecosystem processes.

Ant colony disperses after discovery under bark of pine tree firewood. Likely carpenter ants, *Camponotus pennsylvanicus.*

Emerald ash borer

Insect pests can be detrimental to trees. The **emerald ash borer**, an insect pest from China that feeds on and kills ash trees, has been deemed to have the potential to wipe out ash trees in North America entirely, affecting ecosystem processes as well as plant and animal communities.

Initially discovered in Michigan and southwestern Ontario in 2002, the beetle has killed millions of ash trees to date in parts of southern Ontario and the Great Lake states. It attacks both healthy and stressed ash trees by feeding beneath the bark and disrupting the flow of water and nutrients within the tree's vascular system. If a tree has become infested by emerald ash borers, it will usually die within two to three years.

The emerald ash borer has no known natural enemies to control its spread, which is rapidly expanding. Adult insects are a metallic blue-green with narrow bodies approximately 8.5 to 14 millimeters long. Impacted trees appear to be thinning at the crown, with cracking bark, dead branches and yellowing leaves.

If you see any emerald ash borer or signs of infestation, contact the appropriate authority in your area. To help reduce infestation, do not move infested wood — including firewood, trees, logs, lumber or bark chips — to new areas.

The Asian long-horned beetle, like many invasive pests, has no known natural predators in North America that help contain its spread.

Asian long-horned beetle

Like the emerald ash borer, the Asian long-horned beetle has been found in the U.S. and Canada, affecting several states and two provinces (British Columbia and Ontario). It is a serious pest in its native continent and poses a great risk to Canada's hardwood forests and shade trees, and especially to maple trees, one of the beetles' preferred host species.

Global trade is responsible for bringing the Asian long-horned beetle to North America, by way of infested wood from China used for shipment crates and pallets. The beetle was first detected at U.S. and Canadian ports and inland warehouses in the early 1990s. American populations have been confirmed in New York, Illinois, New Jersey and Ohio. In Canada, the species was confirmed in the Toronto area in 2007 and 2012, and again in 2013. There are restrictions on the movement of potentially infested trees and wood material in impacted areas in an attempt to prevent its spread.

Asian long-horned beetles are a shiny black with prominent, irregular white spots and long black-and-white-banded antennae. Adults are 2 to 4 centimeters in length. Signs of infestation, which you should look for during the summer months, include: round exit holes; oval or round egg sites, which look like small wounds on the tree; the accumulation of frass or sawdust-like material that appears on tree branches or on the ground

as the larvae tunnel and feed; weeping sap; or unseasonable yellowing or dropping of leaves.

After hatching, European gypsy moth caterpillars feed on tree leaves at night for approximately 7 weeks before they pupate.

European gypsy moth

Considered to be a major pest in North America, the European gypsy moth is an invasive defoliating insect that can severely weaken or kill trees. It has been present in Toronto for more than 20 years, preferring tree hosts such as oak, birch, poplar, willow, beech, cherry and elm trees, among others. Rare hosts include ash, catalpa, horse chestnut, London plane and coniferous trees.

The caterpillar or larva stage of the insect eats the leaves of trees, which makes them more likely to contract disease and damage from other insects. The extent of damage can range from light to almost total defoliation depending on the severity of infestation, the health of the tree and other environmental factors. If attacked repeatedly and weakened by other conditions, the defoliation can result in the demise of the tree.

Caterpillars hatch from eggs in mid-spring, feeding on tree leaves nightly for about two months. In mid-summer, the caterpillars pupate in sheltered areas and, about two weeks later, adult moths emerge (usually in early August). Soon after mating, the females lay oval-shaped egg masses.

A European gypsy moth laying eggs.

The caterpillars are a nuisance during outbreaks; infested trees lose their foliage, the caterpillars crawl everywhere and their droppings fall from the trees.

To control the European gypsy moth, remove and destroy any egg masses that you see. Consider wrapping a piece of burlap around the tree stems, folding the band to provide caterpillars with a hiding place during the heat of the day; in the afternoon, collect and destroy any caterpillars you find in this shelter. You may also want to attempt to attract birds that eat caterpillars and moths to your garden by planting appropriate plants such as herbs, flowers and shrubs.

Invasive Plants

Highly adaptable and tolerant of a wide range of habitat conditions, invasive plants are a problem in large cities like Toronto because of the significant disturbance they inflict on the landscape through development, soil compaction and erosion, and pollution. Native vegetation cannot compete with such disturbances, but invasive plants are able to take advantage of these areas, which results in a loss of biodiversity.

Invasive plants possess characteristics that make them especially suited for colonizing new ecosystems. For instance, they have the ability to:

• produce abundant, easily dispersed seeds that can withstand adverse conditions;
• reproduce via multiple pathways, including roots, stems and seeds; and
• release chemicals that inhibit the growth of or kill surrounding native plants.

Common buckthorn

Invasive garlic mustard (*Alliaria petiolata*) covers a forest floor in Illinois

Many invasive plants were brought to North American during European settlement and continue to expand their reach today through the spreading of established communities. Invasive plants located on private properties find their way into parklands — threatening the integrity of natural areas — via wind, wildlife, flooding and garden waste dumping. Due to their aggressive growth habits, many invasive species end up affecting treed areas.

Common buckthorn

Common buckthorn, which inhabits open woods and roadsides, is a European shrub that impacts other species by shading and releasing toxic chemicals. The shrub has small thorns or spines on the ends of its twigs and female trees bear clusters of dark purple berries. Birds and other wildlife spread its seeds when they eat the berries.

Buckthorn seedlings can be pulled or dug out of the ground. Small saplings can be cut close to the base of the trunk, but remaining stumps will have to be repeatedly cut because buckthorn vigorously re-sprouts. To prevent the further spread of the species, make sure to remove the seed-bearing female plants in areas of infestation.

Dog-strangling vine flowers

Garlic mustard

Garlic mustard competes with other woodland species by flowering and seed-setting early in the spring before many native plants begin to grow. The plant's shade has a negative impact on other plants. It is a biennial European species that spreads from seeds. Garlic mustard prefers shaded areas with moist soil, such as floodplain forests and gardens. It produces a low-growing rosette in its first year of growth and forms a tall flowering seed-producing stalk in the second year, with alternate heart-shaped leaves and white flowers. When its leaves are crushed, there is a distinct garlic odor.

Garlic mustard can be controlled by pulling the plant out of the ground or by cutting the plant at its base once it has flowered, before it sets seed in mid- to late-May. This may need to be repeated for several years to target new plants and to deplete the seed bank.

Dog-strangling vine

Dog-strangling vine, also known as swallowwort, is a perennial from Eurasia. The plant can grow up to 6 feet high by twining itself on other plants or structures. Its vines form dense colonies and can smother and grow over small shrubs and trees, with detrimental effects. Preferring sunny areas, the vine has oval, glossy dark-green leaves, purple flowers and fluffy seeds similar to milkweed.

Once it is in full flower, dog-strangling vine can be dug out of the ground. Take care to remove as much of the root as possible. Seeds that have spread in larger patches can be controlled by seed pod removal or frequent mowing.

Wild grapevine

Wild grapevine is an invasive and aggressive deciduous vine that smothers other plants and trees within its grasp. In recent years, it has become a menace across much of Ontario and the Eastern U.S. It is often found along fences, riverbanks and woodlots, as well as in orchards and vineyards. In its quest for sunlight, the vine spreads from tree to tree and will climb over any shrub, tree or fence post that provides support, forming a canopy that blocks enough sunlight to significantly reduce a tree's ability to grow.

It flowers in late spring and early summer, and bears clusters of purplish-black berries (smaller than grapes) in September and/or October, which serve as a food source for wildlife. The vine's leaves are generally the shape of maple leaves and the older stems are covered in brown bark that appears shredded. Wild grapevines, spread primarily through seeds, can also develop roots where the vine touches the soil.

Vines need ample sunlight and can be controlled through tree canopy shading and cutting. Use non-toxic alternatives to herbicides if possible or contact an arborist for serious infestations.

Japanese knotweed

Japanese knotweed is a perennial that grows up to 10 feet high. With stems similar to bamboo, the plant forms dense thickets with white flowers that appear in late summer. Japanese knotweed is found in moist open areas with disturbed soil.

In gardens and residential properties, knotweed stems must be cut down several times throughout the growing season to deplete the root system. Just before flowering — once the plant is 5 or 6 feet high — cut the base of the stalk. Subsequent cutting later in the summer may also be required, as will the need to dig out roots. Cut material should be disposed for landfill garbage pickup to stop it from spreading to other areas.

Norway maple

A European tree species similar in appearance to Canada's native sugar maple, the Norway maple is very tolerant of urban growing conditions and, as such, is a common street tree. It displaces other tree species by offering a large shade canopy, producing abundant seedlings and releasing a toxic chemical that discourages plant growth.

Easily confused with sugar maples, the Norway maple has leaves that range from dark green to dark red in color, and has very dark bark. The trees lose their leaves much later in the fall than native maples. They will grow in any habitat and can easily out-compete native species. Dig any Norway Maple seedlings out of the ground or use hand pruners or loppers to cut small saplings off the base. Consult an arborist about larger tree removals and stump treatment.

Japanese knotweed

Diseases

Diseases in trees and shrubs can reduce the health of the plant, decrease life expectancy and mar the beauty of the landscape. Infectious diseases are contagious and are caused by living organisms called pathogens. Pathogens are parasitic and weaken the host tree by absorbing food from it for their own use.

Fungi are the cause of most tree diseases, but other pathogens include bacteria and viruses. For disease to occur, three conditions are necessary: the availability of a host plant susceptible to infection; the presence of a pathogen; and favorable environmental conditions. By managing one or more of these components, you can reduce the amount of disease in your trees. Temperature and moisture are key factors in disease development. Moisture activates most pathogens and aids their spread, and each pathogen has an optimal temperature range for development. Pathogens are spread by wind, rain, animals, insects and contaminated tools.

While plants respond to infectious diseases in many ways, the most obvious signs of distress appear on their foliage. Fungi are the cause of most leaf diseases. The fungus attacks new shoots and leaves in spring, causing them to turn brown and die. In older leaves, it causes brown patches and premature leaf drop. Fungus spores require moisture to germinate, so the risks are severe during wet springs, but infection is reduced in warm, dry weather. Fungus over-winters on fallen leaves and in cankers on twigs it has killed. Prevention requires cutting out all dead twigs and branches, and raking up fallen infected leaves.

Powdery mildew, rust, leaf spots, scab and anthracnose are all common diseases that affect foliage. Powdery mildew fungus starts as gray or white circular patches on foliage and spreads to become a powdery coating on leaves and stems. It thrives when humidity is high, especially when plants are too shaded or crowded. Symptoms of scab include scab-like lesions on the fruits and foliage of trees that are particularly prone to it, such as apples, crab apples and hawthorns. Trees with these problems need pruning to allow more air movement through the canopy and more light penetration.

Cankers are visible on the branches and trunks of trees. They are the result of a tree's bark and cambium layers dying, followed by the death of the underlying wood. The bark in these areas splits as it dries out and exposes the wood below. Most cankers are caused by fungi; however, sunscald and frost crack can also cause similar wounds. Pruning branches to well below the affected area will help contain the disease.

Vascular wilts are diseases that disrupt the water-conducting elements of the plant, blocking water movement to the crown. Leaves wilt, branches die back and, eventually, the tree will die. One example of vascular wilt is Dutch elm disease, which is spread by the elm bark beetle. The beetle acts as a carrier, transporting the fungus that causes the disease. Therefore, diseased and dead trees must be removed to control the beetle population.

Most Common Diseases

Disease symptoms can be seen throughout the tree on the leaves, fruit, branches and twigs, trunk and roots. Symptoms provide clues that help to identify the disease causing the problem.

1. Twig blight
2. Leaf spots
3. Shoot blight
4. Powdery mildew
5. Canker
6. Fruit rot
7. Wilt
8. Crown
9. Root knots
10. Root rot

Another disease is **verticillium wilt**, a fungus that inhabits a tree's surrounding soil and invades and plugs water-conducting tissue, shutting off the water supply to top growth. Common symptoms are tree wilt and leaves that turn yellow then die. Because verticillium wilt lives in the soil, you should not plant another tree in the same area unless it is a resistant species.

Root diseases are difficult to combat because they are often hidden from sight and access. One common root disease is armillaria root rot, which invades root tissues and forms black, shoestring-like threads just beneath the roots' bark at the base of the tree and produces clusters of mushrooms at the plant's base above ground.

The above information about insects and diseases merely touches upon the wide variety of pest problems that can affect your plants. The key is to be aware of the signs and symptoms you should look for as you examine your trees.

Diseases That Afflict Trees

Apple scab is a fungal disease that affects the leaves and fruit of apple and crab apple trees. The leaves and fruit can develop spots or lesions, causing the leaves to turn yellow, die and drop. The fruit develops brown or black spots and can be irregularly shaped. This is a very common disease and will often cause premature leaf drop, leaving the tree bare in late summer. Cool, wet weather in the spring plays a key role in the degree of infection. Proper culture practices are important in controlling this disease. The fungus over-winters in the leaves on the ground, so rake them up in the late summer and fall each year and dispose of them. Prune the tree to allow for good air circulation and light penetration. When planting, choose an open sunny area with good air movement. Most importantly, choose high-quality, disease-resistant varieties. Crab apple cultivars considered resistant to scab include Malus "Adams," Autumn Glory, Baskatong, Professor Sprenger, Red Snow and White Cascade. The use of chemical fungicides may be necessary for persistent and severe infections. This may involve numerous applications for good control.

Black knot is a fungal disease affecting cherry and plum species. The infection causes hard black swellings on branches and small twigs up to 4 inches long. These black swellings eventually girdle and kill the branch. In late winter or early spring, prune out and destroy the black knot. Cut approximately 2 to 3 inches below the visible signs of the disease, because the fungus may have grown internally below the black knot. Disinfect your pruning tools with bleach after every cut.

Fire blight is a bacterial disease that affects a wide range of plants in the Rosaceae family. This includes serviceberry, hawthorn, cherry, mountain ash, pear and apple trees, among others. Flowers, twigs and branches are affected as they wilt, darken in color, and dry out and die. Dead leaves remain attached to the plant and take on a scorched appearance, which is characteristic of the disease. Fire blight may also extend into the larger branches and the trunk, where cankers form. These cankers are dark, sunken areas with the presence of bacterial ooze on their surface. The disease spreads through rain, wind and insects. To eliminate it, prune all of the tree's infected branches when it is dry and dormant during the winter months. Cut off infected wood at least 1 foot below any discolored tissue or cankered areas. Disinfect your tools with one part bleach to four parts water after every cut, as pruning easily spreads the disease. Avoid excessive nitrogen fertilization, which promotes succulent vegetative growth, and prune lightly to avoid succulent growth as well. Lush, succulent growth is more susceptible to fire blight.

Powdery mildew is a fungal disease that produces a white to gray powdery mold on upper leaf surfaces and young tissue, usually in late summer and early fall. This disease can affect lilacs, rose privets and catalpas, as well as other woody ornamental plants. It commonly appears when warm days are followed by cool nights. Powdery mildew is more of a cosmetic problem and does not damage the plant to any great degree. However, it can be damaging to roses, causing severe deformation. To help reduce the problem, do not overcrowd plants. Plant them in sunny locations where air movement is good. Watering during the day will reduce the spread of the disease, while overhead irrigation late in the day will increase the development and spread of the disease.

Dutch elm disease is a very destructive disease that has killed millions of elm trees in North America. It is caused by a vascular wilt fungus that blocks water flow in a tree until the tree's transpiration is completely cut off. Symptoms include the wilting of large branches and leaves that turn yellow, begin to droop and then fall off. This may begin on one side of the tree. The sapwood becomes stained a dark brown or black and can be easily seen in twigs and branches when cut. Young trees can be killed in a few weeks, while older trees can take a year or two to die. Old, weakened or stressed trees are more

susceptible to Dutch elm disease, which is spread by the elm bark beetle. These beetles carry spores of the fungus from infected trees to the sapwood of healthy trees. The beetles live under the bark of dead and dying elms, as well as in elm logs. Diseased and dead trees must be removed and destroyed to help control the beetle population. Pruning infected branches should be done in the fall rather than in spring and summer, when trees are most susceptible to new infection. A trunk injection treatment, available through trained arborists, may be helpful as well.

Diplodia tip blight has caused a lot of problems in Austrian pines. It also affects most two- and three-needled pines, including red, Scotch, mugo and ponderosa pines. The symptoms of the blight are the death and **flagging** of young shoots. The tips or ends of branches also die. This disease usually attacks pines in an already weakened state. Once again, you can improve tree health and vigor by watering, relieving soil compaction and fertilizing. Also improve air circulation and avoid crowding pines. As well, avoid planting Austrian pines on sites that will be exposed to summer drought.

Cytospora canker is a fungal disease that usually affects trees in an already weakened state from the stresses of poor soil and dry sites. Spruce trees — such as blue spruce, Norway spruce and white spruce — can be affected. The fungus attacks the lowest branches of the tree, working its way upward. The disease enters through wounds or dead branches. A canker is formed that eventually kills the branches by girdling them. Symptoms to look for are pitch oozing from the infected branches or stems and a change of color in the needles that eventually die and fall from the tree. Prune any dead and infected branches in dry weather in winter. Employ good cultural practices to help the tree become stronger and protect it from further spread of disease. Avoid damaging trunk and branches.

Top: fire blight on a plum tree; middle: apple scab; bottom: tape with sticky goop on it to trap bugs (specifically, the elm beetle) to prevent Dutch elm disease.

Rake leaves and twigs under and around affected trees.

Control Measures: Cultural Practices

- Select trees that are resistant to or that can withstand insect and disease problems. Plant resistant varieties.
- Don't overcrowd plants.
- Plant trees in sunny locations with good airflow.
- Disinfect your tools.
- Choose ideal sites when planting trees.
- Maintain healthy plants by providing adequate water and nutrients, as many diseases attack trees that are already weak.
- Reduce moisture by improving drainage and watering your trees properly. Water early in the morning so that your plants are not wet for long periods of time. Do not water late in the day.
- Practice good sanitation. Rake leaves and twigs under and around affected trees. Many insect and disease spores over-winter in the leaf litter. Removing and even burning leaves can help minimize disease spread.
- Consider replacing any trees that require chemical pesticides with a resistant cultivar or a plant that is more suited to the site.
- Prune to allow more air and light penetration through the crown of the tree, which can reduce disease and pest problems. Physically remove

pests by pruning affected growth. For example, cut off a nest of fall webworm or tent caterpillar, prune out black knot from an infected cherry tree or remove dead and diseased branches from a mountain ash infested with fire blight.

- Some diseases require alternate hosts to complete their cycle and do their damage. **Hawthorn rust** is a disease that affects foliage and is characterized by reddish-brown spots on leaves. Juniper hosts and Rosaceae hosts like hawthorn combine to allow disease to spread between them and the hawthorn. In the case of hawthorn rust, the two hosts are the juniper and the hawthorn. Avoid planting different hosts in close proximity.

Control Measures: Alternative Pesticides

If insects and diseases cannot be controlled through cultural methods, consider alternative pesticides that are user friendly and non-toxic.

Insecticidal soap

Insecticidal soap is a contact insecticide, which means that the insects must be sprayed with it directly to be affected. It is effective against soft-bodied insects such as aphids, whiteflies, sawflies, spider mites and scales. The soap disrupts the insects' cell membranes, causing dehydration and death. Foliage is cleaned with soap spray, which removes dirt and honeydew. This improves photosynthesis and reduces the appearance of nuisance insects attracted to honeydew.

Advantage: Insecticidal soap has no residual effect after it has dried.

Disadvantages: The soap has to be sprayed directly onto the insects, so it is difficult to use on very large trees, and it is phytotoxic to horse chestnut, mountain ash and Japanese maple trees (meaning it interferes with gas exchange on the trees' leaves and bark).

Horticultural oil

Horticultural oil works mainly by suffocating insects. It is commonly used in sprays applied before leaf break.

Advantages: It is non-toxic, it kills most insects and it works on over-wintering insects. The insects must be directly hit and it will work on most insects in these situations.

Disadvantages: It can remove blue foliage from evergreens and it can be phytotoxic to certain tree species, such as Japanese maples, amur maples, black walnuts and sugar maples. It may also cause phytotoxicity for plants under moisture stress or humid conditions.

It is important to follow the instructions on the labels of both products and to take care when using them on tree specimens that may be adversely

How to Maintain a Healthy Tree

Most insects and diseases attack stressed trees. While it is impossible to keep all diseases and insects away from your trees, here are a few tips that will help you to maintain a healthy, stress-free tree:

- Water your tree during periods of insufficient rainfall. Nutrients are transported through trees in water, via xylem.
- Do not overwater your tree. This can cause root rot by creating conditions suitable to root-rot fungi.
- Put mulch under your tree. This prevents other plants from growing around your tree.
- Avoid soil compaction, which is often associated with construction activity, as it smothers the roots.
- With the exception of broken limbs, do not remove foliage from newly planted trees. Newly planted trees need all of the leaves they have in order to produce energy.
- Follow recommended pruning techniques. Do not top trees, as it creates entry locations for diseases and insects.
- If fungicides must be used, be sure to apply them using the right method at the right time, and with the right materials. Follow product labels carefully.

affected. The products should always be applied carefully and safely, and according to label directions.

If possible, use the non-toxic remedies as described above.

Control Measures: Chemical Pesticides

If non-toxic remedies have little effect, chemical pesticides may be necessary to control certain persistent insect and disease problems. Fungicides and insecticides should be used only when they are absolutely necessary. Make sure you are spraying at the right time — that is, when the insects are in vulnerable stages — and do not spray needlessly. Limit pesticide use and avoid highly toxic chemicals. Follow all safety precautions. It is best to hire a licensed applicator of chemical pesticides.

In some instances, treatment may not be possible — for example, if the damage has been done and the pest is no longer present, if the damage is insignificant and requires no treatment, or if an effective treatment is not available or permitted.

Remember that plant problems are a part of garden life. Their presence does not always necessitate immediate intervention. Many insect visitations come in short-lived waves triggered by weather and season, such as the first swarm of aphids in early spring. Some fungal diseases are active during damp weather and appear only in particular seasons or in periods of wetness. The objective in pest and disease control is to combat only the problems that stay and increase. Don't panic and be prepared to accept some chewed leaves — the problem will probably disappear soon. In fact, with many insects, natural predators may take care of the problem for you.

Pest Control Common Sense

Shade trees are significant landscape components in any neighborhood. As hosts to birds, squirrels and tree frogs, they endear themselves to those who appreciate nature's array of creatures. Other less-appreciated forms of wildlife, such as fungi, insects, spiders, moths and butterflies, also serve as essential parts of the shade-tree community.

Mimicking the larger ecosystem of the forest that serves as trees' evolutionary home, shade trees accommodate herbivores such as squirrels that eat berries and nuts, mites and aphids that suck plant juices, caterpillars, beetles and flies that eat leaves, and carnivores, including insect-eating birds, insects and spiders that depend on the herbivores for their nourishment.

When one considers a tree's natural habitat, it is misguided to think that that elimination of these organisms is necessary. For perspective, it helps to understand the role that shade tree pests play in the life cycle of a tree, as well as the natural rise and fall of pest populations and the special situation posed by exotic pest invaders.

The Gardener's Guide to Common-Sense Pest Control examines each of these issues, beginning with the relationship between stress and shade tree pests. A tree may show signs of stress when it becomes pest-infested. Thus, it may not produce as many pest-repellent compounds in its leaves or other parts. When pests attack, stressed trees may show a decreased ability to recover. With this in mind, it is useful to assess whether stress can be alleviated or how the tree's vigor can be restored.

Reduce stress through appropriate tree selection. Stresses to shade trees occur as a result of human activities or natural events. When designing your landscape, select appropriate tree species that are native to your area or to similar ecosystems elsewhere, keeping in mind your site's climate, soil, wind exposure and sun exposure. Seek advice from local **arboriculture** experts, horticulturists or garden center staff as to the tree varieties that are the most pest- and disease-resistant in your area.

Reduce stress through proper care. There are numerous ways you can ensure the proper care of your trees.

1. Ensure good drainage. When you plant your tree, the top of the root ball should be elevated 1 to 2 inches above the soil grade to prevent water from collecting around the base of the trunk as it settles. If the base of the trunk is kept moist, it is susceptible to penetration by various disease-causing pathogens. Slope the soil away from the trunk in all directions. Once the tree is established, in about a year's time, remove the berm.

2. If you're staking a young tree, prevent wood damage by ensuring that the ties are flexible and that they permit some movement when the wind blows. This will help the young trunk avoid sustaining bark injuries. Such injuries invite beetle damage or attack by microorganisms.

3. Use proper pruning methods. (See p. 76.)

4. Allow for soil aeration. Tree roots require small empty spaces in the soil to release carbon dioxide and obtain oxygen. Place mulch of organic material over the soil to prevent compaction where human traffic passes beneath the drip line of the tree.

5. Control weeds through proper lawn care, including soil aeration, proper mowing height and frequency, the use of grass species suited to the site, irrigation, and the use of compost, organic or slow-release fertilizers.

6. If needed at all, organic fertilizer or compost should be used to meet the tree's nutrient needs. Overusing nitrogen fertilizer can encourage the growth of aphid and scale populations. A slowly decomposing mulch of leaves and other organic debris often provides the fertilizer that a tree needs. Keep the soil beneath your tree healthy — it will provide for the tree.

7. Protect trees against road salt. Consider selecting salt-tolerant tree species for roadside plantings, such as Norway maple, Scotch pine and red or white oak. Also consider using sand or sawdust instead of salt

to improve traction on your driveway and sidewalk. You should water leaves and branches affected by salt spray from passing traffic to wash away the salt whenever the spray is heavy and again in early spring.

8. Protect trees against natural stresses, such as cold spells and drought, which can reduce tree vigor, by wrapping them to protect against the cold. Periodic deep watering in unusually dry years will benefit any tree.

Even healthy trees experience fluctuating levels of pest problems. These cycles occur throughout the seasons and from year to year based on a variety of factors. These factors include the lag between the appearance and population of herbivorous (plant-feeding) pests and the arrival of their natural enemies and changes in the weather (which may cause high mortality among the overwintering forms of the pest). Practical suggestions in light of such natural cycles include:

- Avoid preventative sprays. It may be a year in which the pest population never becomes large enough to become a problem if left untreated.
- Don't panic when a pest makes its appearance. A small population of pests is tolerable and is actually ideal for birds that may feed the pests to their young. In addition, beneficial insects and spiders will have the opportunity to grow in number.
- Learn to recognize the natural enemies of pests. The authors of *The Gardener's Guide to Common-Sense Pest Control* recommend reading the *Natural Enemies Handbook* by Mary Louise Flint and Steve Driestadt (University of California Press, 1999).
- When faced with an intolerable pest problem, select the least harmful methods of suppression to the pest's natural enemies by using physical and biological controls first: pruning out the nest, crushing egg masses and using water washes.
- Spot-treat or confine treatment of toxic materials to just those areas where the pest problem is intolerable, rather than spraying the foliage of the entire tree canopy.
- Use microbial insecticides (composed of microscopic living organisms) when possible and chemical pesticides only as a last resort. In doing so, the development of pesticide resistance in the insect population will be delayed and the natural enemies of the pest will survive and help combat the pest population in the future.

Magnolia tree

Heavy snowfall and severe winter conditions can have a negative impact on your trees. The key to preventing winter damage is to keep your trees in good health all year long.

6

PROTECTING
YOUR TREES FROM DAMAGE

Construction and Renovation

MANY PEOPLE BUY PROPERTY with the dream of constructing a beautiful home. Often they love the mature trees on the property, which enhance both the look and the value of the lot, and they make plans to build around these trees. Other homeowners may decide to add a new driveway or walkway, or to undertake an ambitious home extension project. In most cases, homeowners do not realize that such activities can have serious detrimental effects on their trees. Without careful planning, trees that are meant to be part of a home's permanent landscape can be needlessly damaged or killed during construction.

Construction involves heavy machinery and equipment that can break, split and tear tree branches, or damage or wound tree trunks. Tools and supplies are often piled up at the base of a tree, causing trunk damage. Contractors unskilled in tree pruning may even remove branches that interfere with the operation of their equipment, leaving poor pruning cuts that may never seal properly.

Unfortunately, much of the damage that results from construction occurs underground, where some of the most serious harm can be done, and is often not immediately detected by unsuspecting homeowners. A tree's root system extends horizontally at great distances in all directions. The absorbing roots contain fine root hairs, located 6 to 12 inches under the soil. Damage to a root system causes serious harm, and can lead to the decline and death of a tree. Typical damage occurs during digging or trenching, when roots are severed or cut, or when a significant amount of the root system is removed. Roots act as stabilizers, providing anchorage and support, and trees can be rather delicate, despite their large size.

If a tree's roots are damaged, some of its branches — or even the entire tree — can die. It is critical to protect roots that lie in the path of construction. Impairment of the root system will affect water and nutrient uptake and could make a tree prone to falling. Signs of stress can be visible within months, or a tree may decline over several years.

Signs of stress from root injury include:

- dieback of the tips of branches, which can result in the eventual death of entire branches, usually from the top of the tree down;
- leaves that become brown and scorched on the edges from lack of water;
- stunted growth and small or off-color leaves;
- excessive suckering or water sprout growth along the trunk and limbs (flower and seed production and water sprout formation are defense mechanisms); and
- early fall color and leaf drop.

Another type of root damage occurs when soil is compacted around the root area of a tree and soil pore spaces are greatly reduced. These pore spaces are important to tree roots because they are filled with water and air, both of which are necessary for tree health. Soil compaction makes it hard for water to infiltrate the soil and drainage is consequently impaired. These effects make it hard for roots to grow and function.

Adding or mounding soil, or changing the grade of the existing soil around a tree, can also cause problems. Roots require air, space and water, so adding soil or changing a grade, even by a few inches, can smother roots by compromising their ability to access air and water.

Prevention of Tree Injury Before and During Construction

Homeowners do have options for ensuring that their valuable trees are not harmed during construction work. Here are some suggestions for a successful landscape protection plan as recommended by the International Society of Arboriculture and other tree-care professionals:

- Usually when homes are built in natural or wooded areas, some trees are cut down to make space for building construction and a few trees are left to surround the home. It is important to understand that these forest trees grew together and protected one another. They grew tall and slender with high canopies because of their proximity to each other. When some of these trees are cut down, it leaves the remaining trees exposed to intense sunlight and their leaves exposed to the wind. A looser canopy means that the remaining trees are susceptible to sunscald on trunks and branches. Plus, trees that grew protected by neighboring trees are now more likely to be damaged by wind and ice loading. You can avoid sun and wind stress by saving groups of trees rather than individual trees.

- Heavily wooded sites should be gradually thinned over a two- to three-year period to reduce the shock to the remaining trees — especially if your property is located within dense pine, spruce or fir forests.
- Mark construction zone boundaries. Ask your builder or architect to mark areas where heavy equipment will be used.
- Make an inventory of the trees on the site. Trees that are over-mature, that display poor form or that have severe insect problems should be marked for removal prior to construction. Also mark trees that need pruning. Select and protect the trees you want to save.
- Erect barriers around the trees, which will help to preserve them. Install temporary fencing such as snow fencing as far out from the trunk as possible. The minimum perimeter should be the drip line, the imaginary line around the tree that follows the edge of the tree canopy.
- Prepare the trees for construction disturbance. Minimize damage by avoiding excavation during hot, dry weather and keep plants watered before and after digging. Prune branches that are dead, diseased, hazardous or detrimental to the tree's shape.
- Limit machinery to one or two well-traveled routes to minimize soil compaction and damage.
- A good temporary measure to reduce soil compaction is to spread a layer of mulch 6 to 12 inches deep in construction areas near trees and along well-traveled routes. This will distribute the weight of heavy equipment more evenly. Don't forget that the mulch must be carefully removed when the work is completed.
- Large roots severed by cutting trenches within a few feet of a tree can remove 25 to 50 percent of its root system. If trenches have to be dug near trees, consider using a tunneling technique instead. Damage to roots will be significantly reduced if tunneling is used. The process is more expensive and time-consuming than trenching, but your trees will be much better off.
- Take great care to sever as few roots as possible and to do so as cleanly as possible — roots that have been cleanly cut regenerate faster than roots torn during construction.
- Not all contractors are concerned about the trees on their job sites. The more protection you have in place, the better. Convey the importance of tree preservation to the people doing the work. You or an arborist should work with the contractor to ensure tree protection.
- Sometimes contractors are allowed to burn waste materials on job sites. Be sure to designate an area well away from your trees, as smoke and heat from fire can cause significant damage to trees.
- Sidewalks and driveways located too close to a tree endanger its health and may threaten pavement stability. Frost heaving, poor drainage and pavement flaws may occur.
- Minimize root disruption by using alternative paving materials. In some communities, brick or flagstone walkways on sand foundations can be substituted for concrete.

Get an arborist involved early, before construction begins. An arborist can determine if a tree situated in close proximity to a construction zone will survive or if it should be removed before the work begins. A skilled tree specialist can also properly prune branches that may interfere with equipment and construction before they are damaged, split or broken. Share your contractor's plans with the arborist so he or she can determine whether work can be done successfully around the specific trees you want to save. Choose an arborist with experience in protecting trees from construction damage.

Horizontal seams

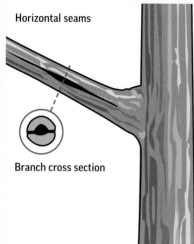

Branch cross section

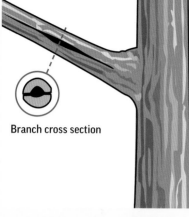

Girdling roots

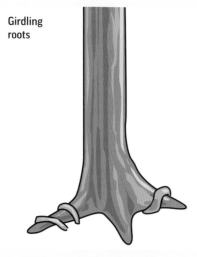

Dead stubs

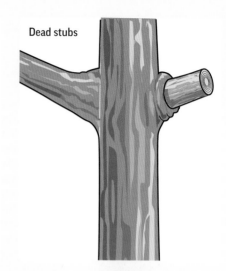

Severe topping

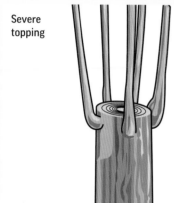

Crowded branches

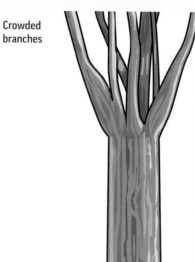

Ground-level wound

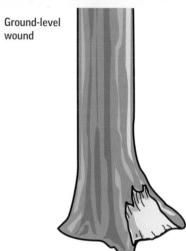

Signs of Tree Damage

Look for defects in your trees as you are gardening or working in your yard in the spring and fall. Always look at potential defects again after severe weather to see if any damage has been done. If a defect is present, you may want to consult an arborist to monitor the progression of the defect or to correct it, if possible. Recognizing tree defects early on can enable you to take corrective measures before the tree becomes a hazard or before removing the tree to prevent damage becomes necessary.

Root rot and tree failure

Canker rot

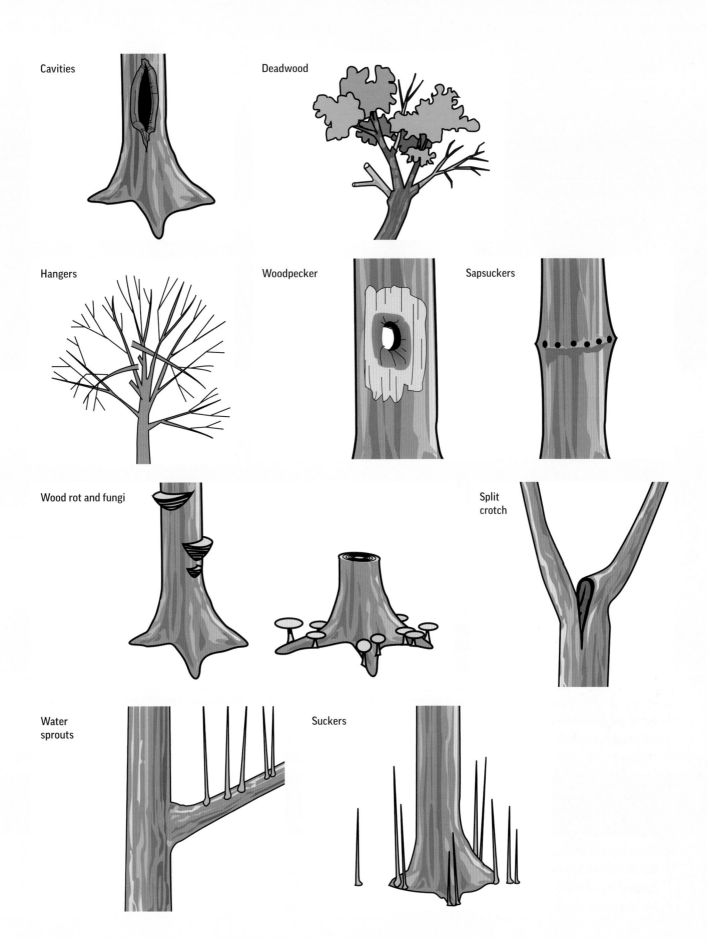

Cavities

Deadwood

Hangers

Woodpecker

Sapsuckers

Wood rot and fungi

Split crotch

Water sprouts

Suckers

amounts of deadwood, excessive dieback and structural defects such as cavities or decay. Some trees may have to be removed, even if preservation efforts were made during the construction period. Monitor your trees' annual growth. A slightly damaged plant will grow more slowly and be less resistant to insects, diseases and weather changes.

- Tree death may occur shortly after construction or even years later. If your tree does not leaf out the following year, it is dead. Large trees should be carefully removed by professionals so as not to damage the remaining plants. Tree loss can have a dramatic impact on site appearance. Prompt replacement will minimize your loss.

Storm Damage and Extreme Weather Conditions

Storms of all shapes and sizes regularly wreak havoc upon trees throughout North America. The greatest dangers during a storm are property damage and physical harm, which can occur when big trees fall. Preparing trees for inclement weather is advisable and should be done well in advance of the stormy season in your area.

Consult a tree professional before the stormy season. Ask the arborist to look for potential hazards, such as stress cracks and weak branches. Examine your trees for the following warning signs:

- electrical wires in contact with tree branches;
- dead or partially attached limbs that could fall and cause damage or injury;
- cracked stems and branch forks that could split and cause the dramatic decline of a tree section;
- hollow or decayed areas on the trunk or main limbs, or mushrooms growing from the bark, which indicate a decayed and weakened stem;
- peeling bark and gaping wounds in the trunk, which indicate structural weaknesses;
- fallen or uprooted trees putting pressure on other trees beneath them; and
- mounded soil at the tree base, which is an indicator of a potentially unsound root system.

Trees are living things and their integrity and stability changes over time. Follow proper pruning techniques to reduce the weight and length of individual tree limbs and to minimize the tree's resistance to wind movement through the crown. Over their lifespan, growing trees will "catch" more wind and become heavier, increasing the chances of limb loss and instability. Power lines, homes and other structures that might not have been threatened a few years ago might suddenly be under threat if a tree has grown substantially.

A tree is bowed to the ground under the weight of ice on its branches.

Ensuring Tree Health Throughout the Winter

In winter, the ground root system of a plant or tree will freeze, stopping or slowing water circulation. Evergreens are at greater risk than other trees, because they keep their needles in the winter. The needles lose moisture to the atmosphere, as well as to the plant itself. Because trees are not able to replenish lost moisture, leaves can dry out and fall off. To minimize the effects of winter drying, high-value evergreens can be treated with wax-like anti-desiccant substances that hold moisture in the leaves.

Snow and ice can become very heavy and can break branches or even topple an entire tree. Pruning your trees can make them better able to withstand the extra weight of ice and snow. Mulch, too, produces a year-round benefit because it increases microbial activity and the fertility of the soil underneath the tree. Mulch has the added benefit of acting as insulation between the root system and the aboveground temperature, which helps to retain moisture in the root system and limit the fluctuation of soil temperature. Ensure that the ground is not yet frozen and has enough moisture before you add the mulch, and make sure that no more than 2 to 4 inches of an organic matter, like wood chips, is used.

Salt used for de-icing streets and sidewalks is harmful to trees, shrubs and grass. You can avoid damage by using only non-injurious types of

Fallen leaves can be beneficial to your soil. While many homeowners prefer a clean and tidy lawn, your soil benefits from this autumnal gift. The leaves are composted over time into nutrients that feed microbes in your soil. In addition, leaves form a natural mulch that suppresses weeds and fertilizes the soil as it breaks down. If you prefer a tidier look, consider raking your leaves into garden beds or using them as mulch around trees.

de-icing salts or avoiding salt applications to sensitive areas. Some specialists believe that you can also reduce salt damage by flushing the soil in treated areas with large amounts of water in the spring.

The severe ice storm of 1998 resulted in damage to many trees in eastern Canada and the northeastern United States. Ice storms are common in the region, so most trees are remarkably resilient. Trees that do not suffer major structural damage, like split trunks, will recover over time. Trees are dormant in the winter and damage at this time of year is less serious than if it occurs during the growing season. If a tree is reasonably healthy and only a moderate number of branches are damaged or removed, the tree should recover and appear normal within a few years.

It is worthwhile to care for injured trees during the dormant season and then wait until the growing season to see if they recover. Many young trees can bend over to ground level because of the weight of the ice collected on their crowns. Trees at this stage of development are quite flexible, and most will recover and regain an upright position when the ice melts.

It is best to wait for above-freezing temperatures to remove ice from trees. Attempting to do remove ice while it is still firmly attached to the tree will lead to bark damage and removal of the buds that will produce new growth in the spring.

Coniferous trees, like spruces and firs, generally suffer much less storm damage than deciduous species. Most coniferous species have narrow crowns and short, upright branches that minimize ice and snow loading. Damage to deciduous tree species is often much more severe. Trees with soft or brittle wood, like Manitoba maples, silver maples, native and European birches, and Siberian elms, are particularly affected. Oak and ginkgo trees, species with strong wood and well-attached branches, suffer less structural damage.

PROTECTING YOUR TREES FROM DAMAGE

How to Protect Young Trees in Winter

Broad-leafed evergreens and young conifers can suffer during the winter, especially from the southern sun's glare and exposure from westerly winds. To protect them, consider erecting a burlap screen in late fall. Be careful that the burlap doesn't touch the foliage and inflict harm and that the plant is not bundled too tightly — in addition to inviting pests and diseases, this can lead to a heat buildup that causes the tree to break dormancy early.

1. Drive three or four wood stakes deep into the ground (approximately 8 inches) around the plant, depending on the size of screen you want (i.e., two-, three-, four-sided).

2. Trim the burlap for height and length. Stretch it around the stables and staple to each from top to bottom, leaving the top open.

3. The screen will protect the plant and allow for good air circulation. When the buds on the tree are visibly swelling, it is generally a safe time to take the screen down.

Don't Let Your Tree Go to Waste

More than 200 million cubic yards of leaves, lawn clippings and branches are generated in urban areas throughout the United States each year. This green waste is expensive to dispose of and could be put to good use.

There is a surprising amount of wood in medium- to large-size trees. An environmentally friendly way to deal with large-size logs or pieces of wood is to have them milled into lumber. Some tree services have portable band saw mills that can be made available on site. Rather than ending up in a landfill, tree trunks can be milled into boards to be used or sold by the homeowner.

Organizations like LEAF (Local Enhancement and Appreciation of Forests) work with the City of Toronto and other stakeholders to use the wood from urban trees in Toronto and southern Ontario. Urban wood comes from trees in urban environments that die of old age, diseases and pest infestations, or that are removed for safety or development purposes. The Urban Wood Utilization Initiative encourages the salvaging and reuse of

Woodlots

IN ADDITION TO PROVIDING the opportunity for enjoyment of wildlife and natural beauty, woodlands on private properties can also be a source of revenue from timber, fuelwood or nut sales.

With proper management and care, a woodlot can yield ongoing benefits. First, remove any dead, dying, diseased or undesirable trees, leaving space to encourage the growth of healthy species. The goal is to obtain the appropriate number of trees per acre that will most effectively make use of the woodlot's growth capacity. For example, an area with too few trees should be managed to promote new growth of desirable species; conversely, areas that are too crowded should be thinned.

Odd-shaped pieces of land unsuitable for crops are often ideal for walnut-planting sites. Black walnut trees are grown for their nuts, as well as for their good quality wood. In areas where climate and soil conditions are favorable, other nut species, such as pecan, hazelnut and almond trees, can be grown.

A woodlot can yield a marketable crop, like fuelwood, in as little as five or six years. To stimulate the growth of trees, as practiced in Norway for centuries, consider coppicing, a process where certain deciduous trees (including birches, chestnuts, hazels, oaks, poplars and willows) are regenerated from stumps. The young tree makes use of the root system of the previous tree and grows more rapidly than it would if it had to establish its own roots. Coppiced birth stumps, called "stools," can nourish new trees for up to 200 years before rooting; in the United Kingdom there are oak trees growing from root systems that are more than 2,000 years old.

Fuelwood can be harvested while thinning a woodlot section, or cut. In general, hardwoods are sold for home heating. Trees grown for timber require many years to reach harvestable size. Good timber trees can result in a high dollar return on the land. With good management, some species can be harvested in as little as 25 years, though the typical timeframe is 60 years.

Mature, good-quality trees can be processed into thin layers of wood used for furniture and plywood. These veneer trees will usually yield more value

If you live in an area with a strong market for Christmas trees, they may provide a solid return on otherwise marginal agricultural land. Bear in mind the time and labor required to provide proper maintenance and annual pruning. Of the more than $1 billion that Americans spent on fresh Christmas trees in 2014, nearly 40 percent went to independent tree farms and nurseries.

Seasoned fuelwood should be dry. This image shows the cracks in logs that indicate dryness.

than trees of lesser quality that can be grown for lumber or posts. In addition, some species can be harvested for pulpwood used for paper products.

The German method of wood stacking, called *holzhausen* or "wood house." The circular form that resembles a beehive, where wood is stacked round and round with irregular-shaped pieces placed vertically inside the pile to create vertical air movement, helps ensure that the wood inside stays dry.

Stack your wood neatly and try to keep it as dry as possible.

If you have to remove a dead or diseased tree, it can be repurposed in many ways, including as furniture.

this valuable resource to create unique wood products.

Based in Toronto, Urban Tree Salvage is Canada's first and largest municipal log salvaging operation. Urban Tree Salvage uses urban forestry waste to design and handcraft one-of-a-kind furniture pieces, including ash tables created from emerald ash borer–felled trees.

Tree companies and landscaping contractors also use wood chippers to chip branches from pruning and removal jobs. Wood chips can be used as mulch around trees or garden beds, or can be composted and used to amend soil for drainage. Consider renting a wood chipper for limbs up to 6 inches in diameter if you plan to do a lot of pruning. It can save time and will provide mulch to use in your garden. Warning: Chippers are very dangerous. It is best to get a lesson on how to operate one. Be sure to wear proper protection when handling a chipper.

Using seasoned, chopped firewood is another alternative to sending wood to landfill, especially if it is burned in modern, clean-burning wood-stoves, which are efficient for heating your home.

Nurse logs, sometimes called "mother stumps," are branches or trunks

Chopped wood should be seasoned for at least a year before it is sufficiently dried and ready to be burned.

that have fallen and remain on the forest or backyard floor, helping the tree's biomass return to the soil. Nurse logs have an afterlife that continues to benefit the soil with nutrients. A well-placed or interestingly formed log or branch can provide visual interest and support other plants while improving the soil. This is another way to make use of wood that might otherwise end up in a landfill.

A tree does not have to be removed just because other parts of it are no longer alive. Provided there is no danger to your property or anyone on it, a dead or dying tree can be a boon to wildlife and an asset to your garden. Trees with wood that resists rot, such as white oak, cedar and locust trees, can stand for many years and are better candidates for habitat than fast-decaying trees such as willows, poplars, cheers or pines. Owls, squirrels and other creatures will nest in the tree's cavities, while beetles, salamanders and tree frogs will use the bark as shelter.

A dying tree can sometimes lead a second life. Known as "Lazarus trees," some trees, including cherries, crab apples, lindens and willows, will sucker out new spouts from the roots or stump after the tree has been cut down; these shoots can be pruned and trained into a new tree.

If dead branches do not pose any danger, they can continue to serve a purpose for birds, insects and other wildlife.

HIRING AN
ARBORIST

7

AN ARBORIST IS A SPECIALIST in the care of individual trees. Arborists are skilled professionals who are trained in the art and science of planting and maintenance. They are knowledgeable about the needs of trees, and are trained and equipped to provide proper care. Hiring an arborist is an important decision for a homeowner to make, because proper tree care is an investment that can lead to substantial return. Well-cared-for trees are attractive and can add considerable value to your property. On the other hand, poorly maintained trees can be a significant liability. Because pruning and removing trees can be dangerous, only those trained and equipped to work safely in your yard should undertake major tree work.

Services Provided

It can take many years to correct improper tree care. Are you willing to take the risk? Good arborists are qualified to provide a broad range of services, including the following:

Pruning

An arborist can determine what type of pruning is necessary to maintain or improve the health, appearance and safety of your trees. Techniques include:

- eliminating branches that rub against each other;
- removing limbs that interfere with wires, building facades and windows, or that obstruct streets and sidewalks;

> ✚ If you own property with trees on it for any length of time you will likely require the services of an arborist. Their unique knowledge and skills are required to provide many specialized services. Arborists have the necessary experience and equipment to safely handle the most challenging jobs. In addition to these skills, they are highly valued for their consulting abilities, reports and assessments, tree preservation knowledge and expert diagnosis, as well as for being able to work in conjunction with landscape architects and other tradespeople.

When to Call an Arborist

Arborists provide a variety of tree-care services including:

- preventative maintenance to keep your tree in good health, which will help it fend off insects and disease problems;
- fertilization and advice regarding the nutritional needs of your tree;
- aeration to improve root growth and alleviate soil compaction;
- cabling and bracing for added support to branches with weak attachments;
- installation of lightning protection systems; and
- spraying or injecting pesticides to control certain insect and disease problems.

Professional arborists ensure that tree branches do not interfere with hydro wires.

- removing hazardous, dead or weak limbs;
- removing diseased or insect-infested limbs;
- removing limbs damaged by adverse weather;
- thinning unnecessary branches;
- creating a better structure that will lessen wind resistance and reduce the potential for storm damage;
- training young trees; and
- improving a tree's shape or silhouette.

Pruning mature trees usually involves climbing into the trees to make cuts. It is not safe to try to prune a tree from a ladder yourself. An arborist will climb into the tree using safety equipment. In addition to general pruning of interfering limbs and dead, dying and diseased limbs, an arborist can also provide specialty pruning such as vista pruning, crown restoration and crown thinning.

Vista pruning involves removing branches to allow a specific view. For example, trees can be pruned to open up a view of the lake from the deck of your cottage. While this type of pruning is meant to provide a view rather than to maintain a tree, arborists will make every effort to minimize any negative effects to the tree's health and appearance.

Crown restoration helps to improve the structure, form and overall appearance of a tree that has been disfigured through severe pruning, vandalism or storm damage. It usually involves pruning gradually over a period of time to help restore the tree to proper growth.

Crown thinning involves the selective removal of branches to increase light penetration and air movement. This type of pruning can help direct desired sunshine onto a backyard pool or patio. Crown thinning also decreases wind resistance and the potential for storm damage.

Tree Health Care and Insect and Disease Management

If you want to reduce pest problems and have healthier trees and shrubs, but do not have the time to tend to your trees, consider hiring an arborist. An arborist can monitor specific woody plants on your property, or all of them. A specialist will be able to identify, record and analyze what is happening with your landscape plants and will be able to detect and treat problems early on before they develop into more serious issues.

This option is particularly helpful if chemical pesticides need to be applied to control certain pests. Arborists involved with plant health care are licensed applicators and will be equipped to safely apply any pesticides. They can minimize the use of chemicals by applying them only when needed and at the right time to maximize effectiveness. Along with chemicals, arborists will use **cultural**, mechanical and biological controls to effectively care for your plants. Combined, these techniques are referred to as **integrated pest management** and form a systematic approach to solving insect and disease problems.

Tree and Stump Removal

An arborist can help decide whether or not a tree should be removed. Tree removal is conducted only as a last resort. It is recommended when a tree:

- is dead or dying;
- is considered irreparably hazardous;
- is causing an obstruction that is impossible to correct through pruning;
- is crowding or causing harm to other trees;
- is to be replaced by a more suitable specimen; or
- must be removed to allow for new construction.

Certain pruning tasks are best accomplished by professional arborists. These include eliminating large branches that rub against each other, removing large limbs that interfere with wires or houses, removing hazardous deadwood and correcting poor V-shaped crotches.

Why Does Your City Prune Ttrees?

Municipal arborists routinely prune trees according to species, age and, in some cases, location. Some of the different types of pruning include:

- **crown cleaning** – the removal of dead, dying, diseased, crowded or weakly attached branches and those weak in vigor from the crown of the tree;
- **crown thinning** – selective removal of branches to increase light penetration and air movement through the crown, and to help retain the tree's natural shape;
- **crown raising** – removal of the lower branches from a tree in order to provide clearance for pedestrians, vehicles, sight lines and buildings;
- **crown reduction** – reduction of the height of spread of a tree, often to make room for utility lines, which is accomplished by pruning back the leaders and branch terminals to lateral branches that are large enough to assume the terminal roles, while maintaining form and structural integrity; and
- **crown restoration** – removal of damaged limbs to restore an appropriate stable form to the tree, often necessary following storm damage.

Your street tree might look bare after being pruned, but it will return to normal during the next growing season with a healthier and more attractive form and structure.

An arborist can remove your tree stump. If not properly removed, excessive sucker growth may result.

Removing large trees is difficult and hazardous work, involving felling techniques and specialized equipment including chainsaws. This work requires an arborist who is skilled and equipped to efficiently remove trees. Never attempt to use a chainsaw without thorough knowledge of its safe use. Learn how to use a chainsaw properly by taking a course. Personal protection equipment must be worn. A chainsaw is a potentially lethal tool that should be used with the utmost concern for safety. Don't attempt it unless you are trained. Better yet, leave it to the experts!

Removing a tree stump requires the use of specialized equipment that can grind the stump down to well below the surface of the soil. Such machinery makes easy work of an otherwise extremely difficult and labor-intensive task. It is worth the money to hire an arborist with the equipment for this job.

Cabling, Bracing and Lightning Protection

Cabling and **bracing** are used to stabilize weak branch crotches and limbs to help reduce the risk of limbs or leaders splitting apart. These tactics may become necessary if young trees are neglected and allowed to mature with structural defects such as co-dominant leaders or branches with narrow crotch angles. Proper pruning when the tree is young will reduce the future need for cabling or bracing. As trees mature, cabling or bracing may become necessary to stabilize and extend their lives. Cabling involves installing flexible steel cables between tree limbs. The cables provide support and limit movement in leaders with poor crotches. They can also support long, heavy horizontal branches. Bracing involves using steel rods

A tree that has a co-dominant stem with included bark, which makes for a weak branch attachment split, probably in the wind, is now a hazard, and should be removed. Have an arborist install cabling and bracing to help keep weak branch unions from splitting apart.

in branches or the tree trunk to provide rigid support. Bracing reinforces weak or split crotches.

A bolt of lightning can blow a tree apart and inflict harm or damage to nearby objects. **Lightning protection** involves installing hardware in a tree to direct the electrical charge away from it. Lightning will strike an air terminal installed near the top of the tree, travel down a copper wire and follow a 10-foot ground rod safely away from the tree. You should consider installing lightning protection for historic trees, trees of economic value, any large trees within 10 feet of a structure, and trees out in the open under which people may take refuge during a storm.

Arborists will recommend these services (cabling, bracing, lightning protection) and properly install the hardware. Installation may not be needed in some situations, so be sure that the advice you receive is consistent with what other tree specialists recommend.

Aeration and Fertilization

Aeration and fertilization are often needed in urban environments. If your soil is lacking in the required nutrients, your tree will show signs of nutrient deficiency. Nitrogen deficiencies show up in the foliage. Leaves may be smaller as growth is reduced and yellowing will occur. This can be corrected with fertilizer. A good application technique is liquid injection, a service provided by arborists. Fertilizer is mixed with water and injected under pressure into the soil. This process applies the fertilizer directly to the root zone, making it readily available for uptake by the tree. Consult your arborist for more information.

Emergency Tree Care

Storms can be harmful and destructive. Arborists can safely remove damaged or weak limbs, or even an entire tree, and prevent further damage to your property.

Planting

Planting the wrong tree in the wrong location can lead to future problems caused by limited growing space, insects, diseases or poor growth. Arborists can recommend appropriate trees for specific locations and plant them correctly.

Bear in mind that some large tree-care companies that have arborists on staff also have research laboratories where they can send soil samples for testing, helping them to diagnose disease and insect problems.

Guidelines for Selecting an Arborist

When selecting an arborist for tree work on your property, consider the following guidelines to make sure you hire the best person for the job:

- Have more than one arborist look at the job and get a written bid specifying the work to be done. Ask if cleanup is required, such as grinding the stump and surface roots, filling topsoil, etc. Ask for and check local references. Ask friends and neighbors for referrals.
- Beware of individuals who want to remove a living tree. This is sometimes necessary, but only as a last resort.
- Be wary of people who go door-to-door offering bargain tree work. Most reputable companies are too busy to do this.
- Low price is a poor gauge of a quality arborist. Often, better arborists are more expensive because they have more specialized equipment, offer more professional help and carry sufficient insurance. The expense of proper care is an excellent investment. Pruning is an art, and skill and professionalism are more important than a low bid.
- Ask for certification of personal, property liability and worker's compensation insurance, then phone the insurance company to make certain the policy is current. You could be responsible for damages and injuries if you hire someone who is not insured.

For any large-tree removal on your property, hire a professionally certified and insured arborist, who will do the job safely and properly.

Determine if the arborist is a member of the International Society of Arboriculture (ISA). Certification is attained after rigorous testing and several years' experience. Certification provides a measurable assessment of an individual's knowledge and competence. Certified arborists must also continue their education to maintain their certification. There are state and provincial chapters of the ISA throughout North America. Membership does not guarantee quality, but lack of membership casts doubt on the person's professionalism. Look for the ISA logo when you are searching for an arborist.

Membership in professional organizations such as the ISA, National Arborists or the American Society of Consulting Arborists demonstrates an arborist's willingness to stay up to date on the latest techniques and developments in this field.

- Some government agencies require contractors to apply for permits and/or a license to undertake tree work. Be sure to comply with any local, state, provincial or national laws. Arborists in your area should be familiar with all such regulations, but double-check yourself.
- Good arborists use only accepted practices. For example, a conscientious arborist never uses climbing spikes unless the tree is to be removed. Avoid arborists who routinely top trees.
- Be wary of the claim of miracle cures.
- The condition of a firm's equipment often reflects its commitment to quality.

Ask questions such as:

- Is your crew trained? Qualified workers are often trade-recognized.
- Will you use specialized equipment such as a bucket truck or crane? Do you own the equipment? If not, ask to see insurance certificates.
- Is tree work your sole source of business?
- How long have you provided services and can you provide references?
- Do you provide a written estimate and is there a charge for the estimate?
- Does the estimate include the cost of brush removal and cleanup?
- When can the work be done and how long will it take?
- Do I have to be home when the work is done?

Items that influence price include:

- the proximity of your trees to hydro lines, landscape features (like pools), driveways and other structures;
- accessibility — for example, it may take less time to remove a tree in the front yard than in the back yard;
- material or debris left on your property, which will reduce time and/or equipment costs;
- additional services such as stump removal, which can require additional visits to the site and increase costs;
- the size of the tree — the larger the tree, the more work it will take to remove it and the greater the costs; and
- the equipment required — the installation of a larger tree requires special equipment and is therefore more expensive, while smaller trees are easier to install.

People walk and ride bicycles along a beautiful tree-lined path on the Yale University campus.

CONTACT INFORMATION

International Society of Arboriculture
www.isa-arbor.com
Phone: (217) 355-9411
Fax: (217) 355-9516
From the website you can enter your zip code, postal code or city to obtain a list of certified arborists in your area. The Canadian chapters of the ISA are Ontario, Quebec, Pacific Northwest, Atlantic and Prairie.

National Arborists
www.natlarb.com
Phone: (603) 314-5380
Fax: (603) 314-5386
Membership comprises commercial tree-care firms.

American Society of Consulting Arborists
www.asca-consultants.org
Phone: (301) 947-0483
Fax: (301) 990-9771
Membership is made up of practicing arborists who specialize in advising, diagnosing, recommending treatments, making appraisals, legal testimony and more.

Your local garden centers are also excellent sources of information and they may be able to refer you to local certified arborists.

ISA CHAPTERS (PARTIAL LIST)

www.isa-arbor.com/membership/localchapters/index.aspx
Please see the list below for websites of international ISA chapters. These websites will assist you in locating a certified arborist in your region.

Atlantic Chapter (Canada – New Brunswick, Nova Scotia, Prince Edward Island and Newfoundland)
For information, e-mail: isa.atlanticchapter@gmail.com

Austria Chapter
For information, e-mail: isa@isa-arbor.com
www.isa-austria.at

Australia Chapter
www.arboriculture.org.au

Brazil Chapter
For information, e-mail: isa@isa-arbor.com
www.sbau.org.br/site/home

Czech Republic Chapter
www.arboristika.cz

Denmark Chapter
(Denmark and Iceland)
www.dansk-traeplejeforening.dk

Florida Chapter (U.S.)
www.floridaisa.org

France Chapter
www.sfa-asso.fr/wordpress

Germany Chapter
For information, e-mail: isa@isa-arbor.com
www.isa-baum.de

Illinois Chapter (U.S.)
www.illinoisarborist.org

Indiana Chapter (U.S.)
For information, e-mail: isa@isa-arbor.com
https://ag.purdue.edu/fnr/associations/IAA/Pages/default.aspx

Italy Chapter
www.isaitalia.org

Kentucky Chapter (U.S.)
For information, e-mail: isa@isa-arbor.com
www.ky-isa.org

KPB Dutch Chapter (The Netherlands)
For information, e-mail: isa@isa-arbor.com
www.kpb-isa.nl

Mexico Chapter
For information, e-mail: isa@isa-arbor.com
www.arboricultura.org.mx

Michigan Chapter (U.S.)
www.asm-isa.org

Mid-Atlantic Chapter
(U.S. – Washington, DC, Maryland, Virginia and West Virginia)
www.mac-isa.org

Midwestern Chapter
(U.S. – Iowa, Kansas, Missouri, Nebraska, North Dakota, Oklahoma and South Dakota)
www.mwisa.org

Minnesota Chapter (U.S.)
msa-live.org

New England Chapter
(U.S. – Connecticut, Maine, Massachusetts, New Hampshire, Rhode Island and Vermont)
www.newenglandisa.org

New Jersey Chapter (U.S.)
For information, e-mail: isa@isa-arbor.com
njarboristsisa.com

New York Chapter (U.S.)
https://nysarborists.com

New Zealand
www.nzarbor.org.nz

Norway
www.trepleieforum.no

Ohio Chapter (U.S.)
www.ohiochapterisa.org

Ontario Chapter (Canada)
www.isaontario.com

Pacific Northwest Chapter (U.S./Canada – Alaska, British Columbia, Idaho, Oregon and Washington)
www.pnwisa.org

Penn-Del Chapter
(U.S. – Pennsylvania and Delaware)
www.penndelisa.org

Prairie Chapter
(Canada – Alberta, Manitoba and Saskatchewan)
For information, e-mail: isa@isa-arbor.com
www.isaprairie.com

Quebec Chapter (Canada)
www.siaq.org/

Rocky Mountain Chapter
(U.S. – Colorado, Montana, New Mexico and Wyoming)
www.isarmc.org

Southern Chapter
(U.S. – Alabama, Arkansas, Georgia, Louisiana, Mississippi, North Carolina, South Carolina, Tennessee, Puerto Rico and the U.S. Virgin Islands)
www.isasouthern.org

Spain Chapter
https://aearboricultura.org

Texas Chapter (U.S.)
isatexas.com

Western Chapter (U.S. – Arizona, California, Hawaii and Nevada)
www.wcisa.net

Wisconsin Chapter (U.S.)
www.waa-isa.org

The **ISA website** has a special site for consumers that provides tree-care information brochures, such as "Tree Values" and "Pruning Young Trees."

Many government bodies offer websites relating to tree care. These include federal sites, such as Natural Resources Canada and municipal sites, such as those by the cities of Chicago and Fort Worth.

Tree Canada, a not-for-profit charitable organization, is a leader in promoting the value of urban forests in Canada. Its website offers information about trees and tree care.
treecanada.ca

PLACES AND ORGANIZATIONS

Here is a list of notable places to see locally native trees.

Adkins Arboretum
Ridgely, MD, USA
(410) 634-2847
www.adkinsarboretum.org

Alaska Botanical Garden
Anchorage, AK, USA
(907) 770-3692
http://alaskabg.org

Alfred B. Maclay Gardens State Park
Tallahassee, FL, USA
(850) 487-4556
www.floridastateparks.org/park/
Maclay-Gardens

UCF Arboretum
University of Central Florida
Orlando, FL, USA
(407) 823-3583
http://arboretum.ucf.edu

Desert Arboretum Park at Arizona State University
Tempe, AZ, USA
(602) 965-8137
https://cfo.asu.edu/arboretum

Arboretum at Flagstaff
Flagstaff, AZ, USA
(928) 774-1442
www.thearb.org

Los Angeles County Arboretum and Botanic Garden
Arcadia, CA, USA
(626) 821-3222
www.arboretum.org

Arboretum
University of Guelph
Guelph, ON, Canada
519-824-4120 ext. 52113
www.uoguelph.ca/arboretum

Arizona-Sonora Desert Museum
Tucson, AZ, USA
(520) 883-2702
www.desertmuseum.org

Arnold Arboretum of Harvard University
Boston, MA, USA
(617) 524-1718
www.arboretum.harvard.edu

Atlanta Botanical Garden
Atlanta, GA, USA
(404) 876-5859
www.atlantabotanicalgarden.org

W.J. Beal Botanical Garden
East Lansing, MI, USA
(517) 355-9582
www.cpa.msu.edu/beal

Beardsley Zoological Gardens
Bridgeport, CT, USA
(203) 394-6565
www.beardsleyzoo.com

Bernheim Arboretum and Research Forest
Clermont, KY, USA
(502) 955-8512
http://bernheim.org

Betty Ford Alpine Gardens
Vail, CO, USA
(970) 476-0103
www.bettyfordalpinegardens.org

Biltmore Estate
Asheville, NC, USA
800-411-3812
www.biltmore.com

Birmingham Botanical Gardens
Birmingham, AL, USA
(205) 414-3950
www.bbgardens.org

Botanica Wichita
Wichita, KS, USA
(316) 264-0448
www.botanica.org

Boyce Thompson Arboretum
Superior, AZ, USA
(520) 689-2723
http://cals.arizona.edu/bta/

Brooklyn Botanic Garden
Brooklyn, NY, USA
(718) 623-7200
www.bbg.org

Cape Fear Botanical Garden
Fayetteville, NC, USA
(910) 486-0221
www.capefearbg.org

Cedar Valley Arboretum and Botanic Gardens
Waterloo, IA, USA
(319) 226-4966
www.cedarvalleyarboretum.org

Cheekwood Botanical Garden
Nashville, TN, USA
(615) 356-8000
www.cheekwood.org

Cheyenne Botanic Gardens
Cheyenne, WY, USA
(307) 637-6458
www.botanic.org

Chicago Botanic Garden
Glencoe, IL, USA
(847) 835-5440
www.chicago-botanic.org

Cincinnati Zoo and Botanical Garden
Cincinnati, OH, USA
(513) 281-4700
www.cincyzoo.org

Cleveland Botanical Garden
Cleveland, OH, USA
216-721-1600
www.cbgarden.org

Crosby Arboretum, Mississippi State University
Picayune, MS, USA
(601) 799-2311
http://crosbyarboretum.msstate.edu

Dawes Arboretum
Newark, OH, USA
(740) 323-2355
www.dawesarb.org

Denver Botanic Gardens
Denver, CO, USA
(720) 865-3500
www.botanicgardens.org

Desert Botanical Garden
Phoenix, AZ, USA
(480) 941-1225
www.dbg.org

Dothan Area Botanical Gardens
Dothan, AL, USA
(334) 793-3224
www.dabg.com

Dyck Arboretum of the Plains
Hesston, KS, USA
(620) 327-8127
http://dyckarboretum.org

Florida Botanical Gardens
Largo, FL, USA
(727) 582-2100

Forest Lawn Cemetery and Arboretum
Richmond, VA, USA
(804) 321-7655

Fullerton Arboretum
Fullerton, CA, USA
(657) 278-3407
https://fullertonarboretum.org

Garfield Park Conservatory and Sunken Garden
Indianapolis, IN, USA
(317) 327-7183
http://garfieldgardensconservatory.org

Botanic Garden at Georgia Southern University
Statesboro, GA, USA
(912) 478-1149
http://academics.georgiasouthern.edu/garden

John C. Gifford Arboretum
Coral Gables, FL, USA
(305) 284-1302
www.bio.miami.edu/arboretum

Graver Arboretum of Muhlenberg College
Allentown, PA, USA
(610) 759-3132
www.muhlenberg.edu/main/aboutus/graver

Green Bay Botanical Garden
Green Bay, WI, USA
(920) 490-9457
www.gbbg.org

Haverford College Arboretum
Haverford, PA, USA
(610) 896-1101
www.haverford.edu/arboretum

Hayes Arboretum
Richmond, IN, USA
(765) 962-3745
www.hayesarboretum.org

Highland Botanical Park
Rochester, NY, USA
(585) 753-7270
www2.monroecounty.gov/
parks-highland.php

Highstead Arboretum
Redding, CT, USA
(203) 938-8809
www.highstead.net

Hoyt Arboretum
Portland, OR, USA
(503) 865-8733
www.hoytarboretum.org

Iowa Arboretum
Madrid, IA, USA
(515) 795-3216
http://iowaarboretum.org

J.C. Raulston Arboretum
North Carolina State University,
Raleigh, NC, USA
(919) 515-3132
https://jcra.ncsu.edu

Edith J. Carrier Arboretum
James Madison University
Harrisonburg, VA, USA
(540) 568-3194
www.jmu.edu/arboretum

Jardin Botanique de Montreal
Montreal, QC, Canada
(514) 872-1400
http://espacepourlavie.ca

Leach Botanical Garden
Portland, OR, USA
(503) 823-9503
www.leachgarden.org

Lockerly Arboretum
Milledgeville, GA, USA
(478) 452-2112
http://lockerly.org

Marie Selby Botanical Gardens
Sarasota, FL, USA
(941) 366-5731
www.selby.org

Mary Grace Burns Arboretum
Georgian Court University
Lakewood, NJ, USA
(732) 987-2373
http://georgian.edu/arboretum

Marywood University Arboretum
Scranton, PA, USA
(570)-348-6218
www.marywood.edu/arboretum

Matthaei Botanical Gardens
University of Michigan
Ann Arbor, MI, USA
(734) 647-7600
www.lsa.umich.edu/mbg

Memorial University of Newfoundland Botanical Garden
St. Johns, NF, Canada
(709) 864-8590
www.mun.ca/botgarden

Memphis Botanic Garden
Memphis, TN, USA
(901) 636-4100
www.memphisbotanicgarden.com

Mendocino Coast Botanical Gardens
Fort Bragg, CA, USA
(707) 964-4352
www.gardenbythesea.org

Mercer Botanic Gardens
Humble, TX, USA
(713) 274-4160
www.hcp4.net/community/parks/
mercer

Minnesota Landscape Arboretum
University of Minnesota
Chaska, MN, USA
(952)-443-1400
www.arboretum.umn.edu

Missouri Botanical Garden
St. Louis, MO, USA
(314) 577-5100
www.mobot.org

Morris Arboretum of the University of Pennsylvania
Philadelphia, PA, USA
(215) 247-5777

Morton Arboretum
Lisle, IL 60532, USA
630-968-0074
www.mortonarb.org

Mount Auburn Cemetery
Cambridge, MA, USA
(617) 547-7105
http://mountauburn.org

Mount Pisgah Arboretum
Eugene, OR, USA
(541) 747-3817
http://mountpisgaharboretum.org

Mounts Botanical Garden of Palm Beach County
West Palm Beach, FL, USA
(561) 233-1757
www.mounts.org

Myriad Botanical Gardens
Oklahoma City, OK, USA
(405) 445-7080
http://
oklahomacitybotanicalgardens.com

Nebraska Statewide Arboretum
University of Nebraska
Lincoln, NE, USA
(402) 472-2971
http://arboretum.unl.edu

New Orleans Botanical Garden
New Orleans, LA, USA
(504) 482-4888
http://neworleanscitypark.com/
botanical-garden

New York Botanical Garden
Bronx, NY, USA
(718) 817-8700
www.nybg.org

Niagara Parks Botanical Gardens
Niagara Falls, ON, Canada
(905) 356-8119
www.niagaraparks.com/niagara-
falls-attractions/botanical-gardens.
html

Nichols Arboretum
University of Michigan
Ann Arbor, MI, USA
(734) 647-7600
www.lsa.umich.edu/mbg/see/
NicholsArboretum.asp

Norfolk Botanical Garden
Norfolk, VA , USA
(757) 441-5830
http://norfolkbotanicalgarden.org

North Carolina Arboretum
Asheville, NC, USA
(828) 665-2492
www.ncarboretum.org

North Carolina Botanical Garden
University of North Carolina
Chapel Hill, NC, USA
(919) 962-0522
www.unc.edu/depts/ncbg

Ohio State University Chadwick
Arboretum and Learning Gardens
Columbus, OH, USA
(614) 688-3479
http://chadwickarboretum.osu.edu

Botanic Garden at Oklahoma State University
Stillwater, OK, USA
(405) 744-5414
http://botanicgarden.okstate.edu

Lauritzen Gardens: Omaha's Botanical Center
Omaha, NE, USA
(402) 346-4002
www.lauritzengardens.org

Orland E. White Arboretum
State Arboretum of Virginia
Boyce, VA, USA
(540) 837-1758
http://blandy.virginia.edu/
arboretum

Overland Park Arboretum and Botanical Gardens
Overland Park, KS, USA
(913) 685-3604
www.opkansas.org/
things-to-see-and-do/
arboretum-and-botanical-gardens

Red Butte Garden and Arboretum
University of Utah
Salt Lake City, UT, USA
(801) 585-0566
www.redbuttegarden.org

Reeves-Reed Arboretum
Summit, NJ, USA
(908) 273-8787
www.reeves-reedarboretum.org

Reflection Riding Arboretum and Nature Center
Chattanooga, TN, USA
(423) 821-1160
http://reflectionriding.org

Reiman Gardens at Iowa State University
Ames, IA, USA
(515) 294-2710
www.reimangardens.com

Royal Botanical Gardens
Burlington, ON, Canada
(905) 527-1158
www.rbg.ca

Salisbury State University Arboretum
Salisbury, MD, USA
(410) 543-6518
www.salisbury.edu/arboretum

San Antonio Botanical Garden
San Antonio, TX, USA
(210) 536-1400
www.sabot.org

Santa Barbara Botanic Garden
Santa Barbara, CA, USA
(805) 682-4726
www.sbbg.org

Santa Fe Botanical Garden
Santa Fe, NM, USA
(505) 471-9103
http://santafebotanicalgarden.org

Sarah P. Duke Gardens Duke University
Durham, NC, USA
(919) 684-3698
http://gardens.duke.edu

Scott Arboretum of Swarthmore College
Swarthmore, PA, USA
(610) 328-8025
www.scottarboretum.org

Secrest Arboretum
Wooster, OH, USA
(330) 263-3761
http://secrest.osu.edu

Sherwood Fox Arboretum
University of Western Ontario
London, ON, Canada
(519) 850-2542
www.uwo.ca/biology/research/
biology_facilities/arboretum.html

Slayton Arboretum of Hillsdale College
Hillsdale, MI, USA
(517) 607-2241
www.hillsdale.edu/about/facilities/
slayton-aboretum

South Carolina Botanical Garden
Clemson, SC, USA
(864) 656-3405
www.clemson.edu/public/scbg

State Botanical Garden of Georgia
University of Georgia
Athens, GA, USA
(706) 542-1244
http://botgarden.uga.edu

Stranahan Arboretum
4131 Tantara Drive
Toledo, OH, USA
(419) 841-1007
www.utoledo.edu/nsm/arboretum

San Francisco Botanical Garden at Strybing Arboretum
San Francisco, CA, USA
(415) 661-1316
www.sfbotanicalgarden.org

Taylor Memorial Arboretum
Wallingford, PA, USA
(610) 876-2649
http://taylorarboretum.org

Toledo Botanical Garden
Toledo, OH, USA
(419) 536-5566
www.toledogarden.org

Toronto Zoo
Toronto, ON, Canada
(416) 392-5929
www.torontozoo.com

Tucson Botanical Gardens
Tucson, AZ, USA
(520) 326-9686
www.tucsonbotanical.org

Tyler Arboretum
Media, PA, USA
(610) 566-9134
www.tylerarboretum.org

UC Davis Arboretum
University of California
Davis, CA, USA
(530) 752-4880
http://arboretum.ucdavis.edu

UCI Arboretum
University of California Irvine
Irvine, CA, USA
(949) 824-5833
arboretum.bio.uci.edu

United States National Arboretum
Washington, D.C., USA
(202) 245-2726
www.usna.usda.gov

University of Alberta Devonian Botanic Garden
Edmonton, AB, Canada
(780) 987-3054
http://devonian.ualberta.ca

University of British Columbia Botanical Garden
Vancouver, BC, Canada
(604) 822-4208
http://botanicalgarden.ubc.ca

University of California Botanical Garden at Berkeley
Berkeley, CA, USA
(510) 643-2755
http://botanicalgarden.berkeley.edu

University of California Riverside Botanic Gardens
Riverside, CA, USA
(951) 787-6962
http://gardens.ucr.edu

University of California Santa Cruz Arboretum
Santa Cruz, CA, USA
(831) 502-2998
http://arboretum.ucsc.edu

University of Delaware Botanic Gardens
Newark, DE, USA
(302) 831-0153
http://ag.udel.edu/udbg

University of Idaho Arboretum & Botanical Garden
Moscow, ID, USA
208-885-5978
http://webpages.uidaho.edu/
arboretum

University of Illinois Arboretum
Champaign, IL, USA
(217) 333-8846
www.arboretum.illinois.edu

Arboretum State Botanical Garden of Kentucky
Lexington, KY, USA
(859) 257-6955
https://arboretum.ca.uky.edu

University of Nebraska-Lincoln Botanical Garden and Arboretum
Lincoln, NE, USA
(402) 472-2679
www.unl.edu/bga/home

University of Wisconsin-Madison Arboretum
Madison, WI, USA
(608) 263-7888
http://arboretum.wisc.edu

United States Botanic Garden
Washington, DC, USA
(202) 225-8333
www.usbg.gov

VanDusen Botanical Garden
Vancouver, BC, Canada
(604) 257-8335
http://vandusengarden.org

Washington Park Arboretum
University of Washington
Seattle, WA, USA
(206) 543-8800
https://depts.washington.edu/uwbg/
gardens/wpa.shtml

GLOSSARY

abiotic plant problem — caused by non-living agents such as weather conditions, soil conditions and man-made physical and chemical disturbances to the air and environment

acid soil — has a pH less than 7

alkaline soil — has a pH of more than 7

annual rings — the rings of wood laid down each year after the burst of spring growth; visible in the cross-section of a tree's trunk

apical dominance — condition in which the bud on the end of a twig or shoot inhibits the growth and development of lateral buds on the same stem

arboriculture — the study of trees and other plants

arborist — a qualified specialist in the care of trees

backfill — soil put back into the planting hole

bare root — a tree with an exposed root system without soil

biotic plant problem — a problem caused by living agents, like insects, and diseases, such as fungi, bacteria and viruses

boring insects — insect larvae, like the European bark beetle, that tunnel under a tree's bark and into the wood

bracing — the installation of metal rods through weak portions of a tree for added support

branch collar — the area where a branch joins another branch or trunk, sometimes identified by swelling where the branch meets the trunk

branch union/crotch — a point where a branch originates from the trunk or another branch

bud — a small protuberance on the stem of a plant that may develop into a flower or shoot

cabling — the installation of hardware in a tree to help support weak branches or crotches

caliche — soil that is heavy in alkalies

caliper — measurement of the diameter of a tree's trunk

callus — the tissue formed by the cambium layer around and over a wound

candles — light-colored and soft new growth on the branch ends of evergreens

canker — a localized diseased area, often shrunken and discolored, on a tree's trunk and branches

central/dominant leader — the main stem of a tree

chemical pesticide — a control measure used to combat persistent insect and disease problems, sometimes toxic

chewing insects — also called defoliators and leaf miners, these are insects like the gypsy moth that eat plant tissue

chlorophyll — a green pigment concentrated in outer leaf tissues

CODIT — compartmentalization of decay in trees. A natural defense in trees by which they wall off decay in the wood

competing leader — a stem competing with the central stem of a tree

complete fertilizer — a fertilizer that contains nitrogen, phosphorus and potassium

conifer — a cone-bearing tree such as a pine, spruce or cedar

controlled-release fertilizer — a fertilizer made up of soluble granules encased within a permeable coating and that are released through watering

cork/bark cambium — layers of cells that give rise to the cork and bark

corrective pruning — an activity that involves pruning interfering limbs, poorly spaced limbs and weak crotches

cracks — defects in a tree that may pose a risk of tree or branch failure

crown — the aboveground portions of a tree (also referred to as the canopy)

crown restoration — a method of restoring the natural growth habit of a tree that has been topped or damaged in a storm

cultivar — a tree cultivated to produce specific desirable features such as foliage color and height

cultural control — a method of controlling plant problems by providing a growing environment that is favorable to the host plant and/or unfavorable to the pest

deciduous — trees and shrubs that shed all of their foliage during autumn to prepare for dormancy during winter

dieback — any plant part that is dying, usually the ends of branches

dormant — a state of reduced physiological activity in the organs of a plant

drip line — the perimeter of the area under a tree's crown

dwarf tree — a tree that is smaller than the usual size for a particular species

evergreen — trees and shrubs that keep their green foliage throughout the year

fertilizer — a substance added to a plant or its surrounding soil to increase the supply of essential elements

flagging — a dead, dropping branch with discolored foliage

foliage — the leaves of a plant

flush cut — the removal of a branch right to the trunk, leaving no stub, which removes the natural protection zone of a tree

girdling — inhibiting the flow of the water and nutrients in a tree by "choking" the tree's root tissues

girdling roots — roots located above or below ground level whose circular growth around the base of the trunk or over individual roots applies pressure to the bark area, thereby choking or restricting the flow of water and nutrients

glazing — occurs when the sides or bottom of the planting hole become smooth, forming a barrier through which water has difficulty passing

graft — a shoot or bud of one plant inserted into the stem or trunk of another

guying — securing a tree with ropes or cables fastened to stakes in the ground

hardiness zone rating — the accepted standard of determining the hardiness of a particular plant

hardiness zone — the preferred growing conditions of a particular plant

hawthorn rust — a disease that affects foliage and is characterized by rusty spots on leaves

heartwood — non-functional xylem tissues that help support a tree's trunk

heat island effect — a phenomenon caused when the sun beats down on concrete and asphalt in the city, increasing temperatures by up to 9 degrees

honeydew — a sticky, sugary secretion deposited on leaves and stems by insects such as aphids and whiteflies

horticultural oil — a non-toxic alternative pesticide

included bark — bark that is pushed inside a developing crotch, causing a weakened structure

insecticidal soap — a non-toxic insecticide soap spray

integrated pest management — a systematic approach to insect and disease management

interfering limbs — limbs that cross each other or rub against one another

lac balsam — a natural substance used as a cosmetic repair to trunk damage resulting from broken or torn limbs

lateral branch — a secondary branch

leach — the tendency for elements to wash down through the soil

leaf scorch — the browning or shriveling of foliage, usually caused by drought where sunshine and drying winds stimulate water loss from leaves

lenticels — elongated pores in a tree's bark that permit the exchange of gases

lightning protection — the installation of hardware in a tree to direct electrical charges away from it

lion tailing — stripping branches of their lateral limbs, leaving growth only on the ends of the branches

microclimate — areas within a garden where the climate is modified; warm microclimates, usually near tall trees, hedges, fences and walls, are sometimes suitable for tender or out-of-zone plants.

mulch — an organic matter, like wood chips, spread on the ground around trees to prevent the evaporation of water and to provide insulation against the cold

mycorrhizae — a fungus that forms a symbiotic relationship with a tree's roots

native species — a species that is indigenous to a region

oasis effect — a phenomenon caused when wind moves through a shade canopy or stand of trees, cooling the air under the trees by as much as 10 degrees

out-of-zone — a tree planted in an area outside of its optimum hardiness zone

photosynthesis — a process by which light energy is used to combine carbon dioxide and water to produce sugar and oxygen

pith — the central core of early growth in twigs

phloem — a thin layer of cells inside bark that carries carbohydrates produced by leaves to all of the plant's living tissue

pH — a measure of acidity or alkalinity in soil

powdery mildew — white, powdery patches caused by a certain fungus that appear on leaves if they become overcrowded and the soil is dry

primary nutrients — nitrogen (N), phosphorous (P) and potassium (K)

prune — to purposefully cut and remove parts of a tree for a specific reason

root ball — the containment of roots and soil of a tree

root bound — a condition of roots of trees that have been grown in pots with inadequate room for root growth and movement

root burn — a condition of roots of trees that have been grown in pots with inadequate room for root growth and movement

root collar — a marked swelling of the tree trunk usually seen at or near the ground line

sapwood — the outer wood that transports water, oxygen and minerals from a tree's roots to its leaves

scaffold branches — the permanent or structural branches of a tree

secateurs — bypass-style pruning shears used on small trees and shrubs to make cuts up to a ½ inch in diameter

shade tree — a large tree, usually deciduous, that provides ample shade as a result of its size

shearing — removing a portion of the current season's growth on a shrub

skeletonizing — the removal of leaf tissues between the leaf veins

soil amendment — a material added to soil to improve its physical or chemical properties

soil analysis — the laboratory analysis of soil to determine its pH and mineral composition

soil compaction — soil compressed by heavy equipment or other means, resulting in the reduction of total pore space

stomata — tiny pores in leaves that allow gases to be exchanged

stub — what remains of a branch after it's been cut

sucker — a shoot arising from the base of a tree

sucking insect — insects, such as aphids and mites, that penetrate and feed on plant juices by sucking out sap

sunscald — a condition that occurs when living bark tissue dehydrates and dies from exposure to bright, intense winter sun, or when water in thawed bark cells refreezes and expands at night, destroying the cells

thinning — selectively removing unwanted branches and limbs to provide light and air penetration through the tree or to lighten the weight of the remaining limbs

topping — cutting back a tree to buds, stubs or laterals not large enough to assume dominance

transplanting — moving a plant to a new location

tree spade — a mechanical device used to dig up and move trees

upright branches — branches that grow straight up rather than outward

U-shaped crotch/fork — a stronger branch union than a V-shaped crotch

V-shaped crotch/fork — a poor branch attachment or co-dominant stem; a weak crotch is likely to have included bark (common in silver maple)

vascular tissues — tissues that conduct water or nutrients

vertical mulching — a method used to relieve compacted soil, which involves drilling holes every few feet to a depth of approximately 12 inches and backfilling them with organic matter like peat moss

verticillium wilt — a fungus that inhabits the soil surrounding a tree and invades and plugs the tree's water-conducting tissues, shutting off the water supply to top growth

vista pruning — removing branches to allow for a specific view (like the view of a lake from a cottage deck)

water sprout — a secondary, upright shoot arising from the trunk or branches of a plant

xylem — a tissue that transports water, oxygen and nutrients up from the tree's roots to its branches and leaves

REFERENCES

In writing this book, we relied heavily on information provided by the International Society of Arboriculture, especially the tree-care information brochures, the *Arborists' Certification Study Guide* and the *Bartlett Tree Experts Course in Arboriculture.*

Adam, Judith. *Landscape Planning: Practical Techniques for the Home Gardener.* Toronto, ON: Firefly Books, 2002.

Appleton, Bonnie Lee. *Rodale's Successful Organic Gardening: Trees, Shrubs and Vines.* Emmaus, PN: Rodale Press, 1993.

Bartlett Tree Experts Course in Arboriculture. Bartlett Tree Research Laboratories in cooperation with the International Society of Arboriculture, Bartlett Tree Research Laboratories, Charlotte, NC, 1999.

Benvie, Sam. *The Encyclopedia of Trees: Canada and the United States.* Toronto, ON: Key Porter Books, 1999.

Borenstein, Seth, "Three Billion Trees on Earth: Scientists Find, but More Needed," *Toronto Star,* September 2, 2015, https://www.thestar.com/news/world/2015/09/02/3-trillion-trees-on-earth-scientists-find-but-more-needed.html.

Bredenberg, Jeff. *How to Cheat at Gardening and Yard Work: Shameless Tricks for Growing Radically Simple Flowers, Veggies, Lawns, Landscaping, and More.* New York, NY: Rodale Books, 2009.

Brochures prepared by the Council of Tree and Landscape, developed by the International Society of Arboriculture, 1994: Benefits of Trees, Buying High-Quality Trees, Insect and Disease Problems, Mature Tree Care, Plant Health Care Recognizing Tree Hazards, Treatment of Trees Damaged by Construction, Tree Selection, Tree Values, Why Hire an Arborist, Why Topping Hurts Trees.

Bruce, Ian. "Standard Pruning" and "Hazard Tree Management" course notes, Humber College, Toronto, ON, 1996.

Buchanan, Rita. "Caring for Your Trees." *Country Living Gardener,* October 2000, 8, no. 5, 93–100.

Carbon, Chris R. "Mulch, Park 2: Go Wide, Not Deep." *International Society of Arboriculture Arborist News,* II, no.1 (2002): 35–39.

"City Trees: How to Plant a Tree." Chicago Dept. of Environment, 1998.

"Controlling Invasive Plant Species – Tree Maintenance – Trees & Ravines." City of Toronto, 1998–2015, http://bit.do/invasive-plants

Cole, Trevor. *Gardening with Trees and Shrubs in Ontario, Quebec, and the Northeastern U.S.* Vancouver/Toronto: Whitecap Books, 1996.

Cullen, Mark, "Tree Helps You Breathe Easier: Some Thought in the Short Term to Tree Planting: A Purchase with Long-Term Benefits," *Toronto Star,* September 5, 2015.

Cunningham, Linda Raglan. *Complete Guide to Trees and Shrubs.* Des Moines, IA: Meredith Books, 2004.

Dirr, Michael A. *Manual of Woody Landscape Plants: Their Identification, Ornamental Characteristics, Culture, Propagation and Uses.* Champaign, IL: Stipes Publishing L.L.C., 1998.

Farrar, John Laird. *Trees in Canada.* Fitzhenry & Whiteside Limited and the Canadian Forest Service Natural Resources Canada in cooperation with the Canada Communication Group – Publishing Supply and Services Canada, Markham, ON, 1995.

Fitzpatrick, Mike. "Protect Trees and Increase Property Value with Tree Preservation." *International Society of Arboriculture Arborist News,* Volume II Number 3 (2002): 58–60.

Heimann, M.F., O.S.F Boone, and D.M. Boone, "Disorder: Black Knot Plum and Cherry," St. Louis Park, MN: Rainbow Treecare, n.d.

Hessayon, Dr. D.G. *The Tree and Shrub Expert.* London: Transworld Publishers, 2001.

Ho, Wendy, "Canada's Old-Growth Forests an Environmental Treasure," *The Huffington Post Canada,* September 24, 2015, http://www.huffingtonpost.ca/the-nature-conservancy-of-canada/old-growth-forests-canada_b_8136252.html.

Hole, Jim. "Prudent Pruning," *National Post,* April 7, 2001, W22.

Hole, Lois. *Lois Hole's Favorite Trees and Shrubs.* Edmonton, AB: Lone Pine Publishing, 1997.

"How to Manage Woodlots and Tree Plantations." Arbor Day Foundation, https://www.arborday.org/programs/graphics/conservation-trees/woodlots-tree-plantations.pdf.

"How Trees Fight Climate Change." Arbor Day Foundation, www.arborday.org/globalwarming/treeshelp.cfm.

Hume, Christopher, "May Be Nature, but It's Not Natural," *Toronto Star,* June 6, 2004.

"Invasive Species." U.S. Forest Service Pacific Northwest Research Station, http://www.fs.fed.us/pnw/invasives.

Ip, D.W. Forestry Leaflet 19: Dutch Elm Disease, Forestry Canada, Ministry of Supply and Services Canada, 1992.

Johnson, Gary R. "Protecting Trees from Construction Damage: A Homeowner's Guide." Regents of the University of Minnesota, 1999, http://www.extension.umn.edu/garden/yard-garden/trees-shrubs/protecting-trees-from-construction-damage.

Johnson, Jan and John C. Fech. *Ortho's All about Trees.* Des Moines, IA: Meredith Books, 1999.

Justin Gillis, "Delegates at Climate Talks Focus on Saving the World's Forests," *New York Times,* December 10, 2015, http://www.nytimes.com/2015/12/11/world/delegates-at-climate-talks-focus-on-saving-the-worlds-forests.html?_r=0.

Kershaw, Linda. *Trees of Ontario.* Edmonton, AB: Lone Pine Publishing, 2001.

Kessell, Christopher. "Juniper & Diplodia Tip Dieback." Ontario Ministry of Agriculture, Food & Rural Affairs, *OSTC News,* II, no. 3 (summer 1994).

"Landscape Trees and Climate Change." Michael Kuhns, Utah State University, 2015, http://forestry.usu.edu/htm/city-and-town/urbancommunity-forestry/landscape-trees-and-climate-change.

Lily, Sharon J. *Arborists' Certification Study Guide*. Sharon J. Lilly, Champaign, IL: International Society of Arboriculture, 2001.

MacMahon, Eamon, "Amazon of the North: It's the World's Largest Storehouse of Carbon and Unfrozen Fresh Water. Why Canada Must Give the Boreal Forest Room to Breathe," *The Walrus*, November 2011, http://thewalrus.ca/amazon-of-the-north.

Meyer, Robinson, "The Best Technology for Fighting Climate Change? Trees," *The Atlantic*, February 9, 2015, http://www.theatlantic.com/technology/archive/2015/02/the-best-technology-for-fighting-climate-change-trees/385304.

Mullard, Asher, "Run, Forest, Run: Helping Trees Flee Climate Change," *The Walrus*, November 16, 2015, https://thewalrus.ca/run-forest-run.

Murray, Joan. *Tom Thomson: Trees*. Toronto: McArthur and Company, 1999.

Mytting, Lars. *Norwegian Wood: Chopping, Stacking, and Drying Wood the Scandinavian Way*. New York, NY, Harry N. Abrams, 2015.

Nursery & Landscape Plant Production, Publication 383, Ontario Ministry of Agriculture, Food and Rural Affairs, 2000.

Obrizok, Robert A. *A Garden of Conifers: Introduction and Selection Guide*. Deer Park, WI: Capability's Books, 1994.

Olkowski, William, Sheila Daar, and Helga Olkowski. *The Gardener's Guide to Common-Sense Pest Control*. Newtown, CT: The Taunton Press, Inc., 2013.

Ontario Extension Notes "Maintaining Healthy Urban Trees," Land Owner Resource Centre, http://www.lrconline.com/Extension_Notes_English/pdf/urbntrs.pdf.

Osborne, Robert. *Hardy Trees and Shrubs: A Guide to Disease-Resistant Varieties for the North*. Toronto, ON: Key Porter Books, 1996.

O'Sullivan, Penelope. *The Homeowner's Compete Tree and Shrub Handbook: The Essential Guide to Choosing, Planting, and Maintaining Perfect Landscape Plants*. North Adams, MA: Storey Publishing, 2007.

Pirone, P.P., J.R. Hartman, M.A. Sail, and TP. Pirone. *Tree Maintenance*. New York, NY: Oxford University Press, 2001.

Roddick, Christopher and Beth Hanson. "The Tree Care Primer: Handbook #186". *Brooklyn Botanic Garden, Inc.*, 2007.

Saunders, Doug, "Green surprise: Why the World's Forests Are Growing Back," *Globe and Mail*, August 29, 2015, http://www.theglobeandmail.com/opinion/we-are-making-the-globe-greener/article26147272.

Smiley, Thomas, Sharon Lilly, and Patrick Kelsey. "Fertilizing Trees and Shrubs Part 1: Determining if, When, and What to Use." *International Society of Arboriculture Arborist News*, II, no. 2 (2002): 17–22.

"Some Tips on How to Care for Damaged Trees." Canadian Forest Service, Natural Resources Canada.

Sternberg, Guy, and Jim Wilson. *Landscaping with Native Trees: The Northeast, Midwest, Midsouth and Southeast Edition*. Shelbourne, VT: Chapters Publishing Ltd., 1995.

"Stewardship Notes." Indiana Division of Forestry, http://www.in.gov/dnr/forestry/files/grapevines.pdf.

Stienstra, Ward. "Apple Scab," Plant Pathology, AG-FS-1173, Minnesota Extension Service, University of Minnesota, n.d.

"Sustaining and Expanding the Urban Forest: Toronto's Strategic Forest Management Plan." City of Toronto, Parks, Forestry and Recreation, Urban Forestry, 2013, http://www.toronto.ca/legdocs/mmis/2013/pe/bgrd/backgroundfile-55258.pdf.

–, and Dale R. Bergdahl. "Spruce and Their Diseases." University of Minnesota, n.d.

Sunset Books and Sunset Magazine eds. *Sunset Trees and Shrubs: A–Z Encyclopedia, Planting and Care, Plant Selection Guide*. Menlo Park, CA: Sunset Publishing Corporation, 1994.

Tanenbaum, Frances, ed. *Taylor's 50 Best Trees: Easy Plants for More Beautiful Gardens*. Boston, MA/New York, NY: Houghton Mifflin Company, 1999.

"Threats to Trees — Tree Maintenance — Trees & Ravines." City of Toronto, http://bit.do/treethreats.

"Tree Pruning." City of Ottawa, http://ottawa.ca/en/residents/water-and-environment/trees-and-community-forests/tree-pruning.

Tucker, Patrick J. "Arboriculture — Chapter IV" of Horticulture I, course #191 (1991), Independent Study division, University of Guelph, Guelph, ON.

Urban, James. *Up By Roots: Healthy Soils and Trees in the Built Environment*. Champaign, IL: International Society of Arboriculture, 2008.

Ontario Ministry of Natural Resources, Ontario Commercial Arborist Association and City of Toronto. *You Need to Know about the Management of the Emerald Ash Borer (EAB): Guidelines for hiring tree care services to manage urban trees*. Toronto, ON: City of Toronto, 2012.

White, Hazel. *Small-Tree Gardens: Simple Projects, Contemporary Designs*. San Francisco, CA: Chronicle Books, 2000.

Whitman, Ann H., *ed. National Audubon Society Pocket Guide: Familiar Trees of North America East*. New York, NY: Alfred A. Knopf, 1986.

ACKNOWLEDGMENTS

We are grateful to our editor and the staff at Firefly Books for developing this book.

We thank Patricia Thomson for reviewing the manuscript.

We also wish to acknowledge our teachers, especially those at the University of Guelph, Humber College and Simon Fraser University.

PHOTO CREDITS

Illustrations by **John Lightfoot Peters**

All photographs by **Daniel Prendergast**, **Mai Prendergast** and **Erin Prendergast** with the exception of the following:

Shutterstock
cover (top left, top center, top right), back cover (bottom, top center) pp. 2, 6, 10, 12, 14, 15, 17, 18, 19, 37, 45, 61, 67, 74, 75 (left), 101 (left), 103, 105, 106, 107, 109, 110, 111, 115, 116, 121, 128, 129, 131, 134 (bottom), 138, 140, 142, 147

iStock
cover (bottom), back cover (top left), pp. 29 (top right, middle left), 48, 108

Dreamstime
pp. 68, 75 (right)

p. 101 **Cheryl Moorehead**, Bugwood.org (top right), **Steven Katovich**, USDA Forest Service, Bugwood.org (bottom right)

p. 104 courtesy **Stephen Smith**, Urban Forest Associates Inc., except top left, courtesy **Amandeep Tiwana**, Bartlett Tree Services Toronto

p. 107 (bottom) courtesy **Amandeep Tiwana**, Bartlett Tree Services Toronto

INDEX